CUT & SEW

CUT & SEW

Working with Machine-Knitted Fabrics

Pam Turbett

B.T. Batsford Ltd.   London

To Gwen, my mother

ISBN 0 7134 4409 6

Typeset by Santype International Ltd., Salisbury, Wilts.
and printed in Great Britain by
Anchor-Brendon Ltd
Tiptree Essex
for the publishers
B.T. Batsford Ltd.
4 Fitzhardinge Street
London W1H 0AH

ACKNOWLEDGMENTS

My very grateful thanks to: Peter and Pat Welsh and all the staff at Sewing Machine Supplies and Swiftknitters, Portsmouth, who started me off, encouraged me on, knitted fabrics for me and answered my innumerable questions; Ann Taylor, for endless help and advice and for widening my experience of the machine-knitting world; Hazel Ratcliffe, who gave me permission to include some of my writing already published in *Knitting Machine Digest*, and who enabled me to meet Kathleen Kinder and Dorothy Gill, who both helped with valuable information and advice; Santina Levey of the Department of Textiles and Dress at the Victoria and Albert Museum, for historical notes; Pat Beaumont of the Vilene Organisation, Eve Petty of Toyota Sewing and Knitting, Pat Carlow of Butterick Fashion Marketing Co. (U.K.) Ltd and Michael Quitmann of Frister + Rossmann, for photographs and information; Vogue/Butterick and Simplicity/Style for permission to use photographs of designs derived from their patterns; all the other importers, manufacturers and suppliers listed on pp. 113–6 for their help in the form of illustrations and information.

I would also like to thank Val Porter for her impeccable typing of my text and her very professional advice.

Colour photography by Virginia Turbett
Black-and-white photographs by John Coombs and Virginia Turbett
The models in the colour photographs are Mandy Coombs and Patricia Turbett
All other work by the author except where otherwise stated

Contents

Introduction

My first attempt at cut-and-sew must have been in 1943. As Wrens working on a bleak and chilly Scottish signal station, we were issued with 'passion killers' to keep our nether regions warm. These were appropriately navy blue and rib-knitted in pure wool, unlike the regulation 'blackouts' which were voluminous and made of rayon lock-knit. Whilst being grateful to their Lordships of the Admiralty for their concern, we found them not only scratchy but distinctly bulky on the hips—so we rapidly devised a way of chopping up the inside-leg seams, turning the whole thing upside-down and converting it into a rather smart, boat-necked, sleeveless pullover!

Since then, without ever having heard (until comparatively recently) of the term *cut-and-sew*, I have altered innumerable badly fitting sweaters and done a great deal of dressmaking with purchased knitted fabrics in every kind of weight and texture. The world of domestic machine-knitting came as a revelation, only a few years ago, when I discovered that it is actually possible to design and create one's own fabrics at home.

Cut-and-sew is probably as old as knitting and scissors. The Victoria and Albert Museum has an example of the knitted caps with elaborate brims which were worn from the late fifteenth century onwards (fig. 1).

Fig. 1 *Cut-and-sew hat—fifteenth-century (Victoria and Albert Museum, Crown Copyright)*

Fig. 2 *Cut-and-sew hat—twentieth-century: 1 strand of 4-ply Shetland, cut on a Very Easy Vogue pattern, lined and interlined, top-stitched*

They were heavily felted, cut and seamed. There are obvious parallels with the modern cut-and-sew hat shown in fig. 2. The V & A also has a little white cotton jacket, typical of those worn by children and adults in the seventeenth and early eighteenth centuries; these were knitted in the round and then cut up the front, the raw edges turned in and hemmed (fig. 3). Framework knitters in the eighteenth century produced pieces for waistcoats which were then made up by cut-and-sew methods, but in the early nineteenth century they were complaining that their skilled work in the making of fully-fashioned hosiery was being replaced by the speedier, more profitable cut-and-sew version. (See Kathleen Kinder's Resource Books and *Techniques in Machine Knitting*.) They called them 'spurious articles' and I, for one, would agree that seamless socks and stockings must be superior and more comfortable to wear; a clear case of the unsuitable use of cut-and-sew methods!

I do not want to suggest that the skills involved in making beautiful fully-fashioned knitwear should be cast aside in favour of what, for centuries, has been used by manufacturers as a cheaper, faster way of doing it. I want to encourage you to make something quite different from knitwear: clothes which are more structured, sharper and clearer in line with a purposefully-cut look; possibly more formal (although they should not be less comfortable to wear) and combining the best skills of machine-knitting, dressmaking and tailoring.

Cut-and-sew is not the fiendishly difficult and hazardous craft that the uninitiated imagine it to be. The knitting does *not* disintegrate as soon as it is cut, and sewing it is simple as soon as a few basic rules about pressing and stabilising have been mastered.

Of course, there are ways of designing and producing your own fabric, or pieces, (partially shaped or fully shaped) at home, other than on a domestic knitting machine. If, like me, you cannot watch television without *doing* something, you could be hand-knitting, crocheting, or using Dr. Patrick Riley's 'Simple-Frame', which is both quieter and less expensive than most knitting machines. (The problem with the last is that it is used mainly with chunky yarns and produces a very stretchy fabric, but the use of knit-weaving, or of a Fair Isle pattern, plus pressing and interfacing, should make a suitable fabric.) Tunisian crochet is a beautifully firm medium for cut-and-sew and, as shaping is easy, wastage is minimal.

The message of this book is really

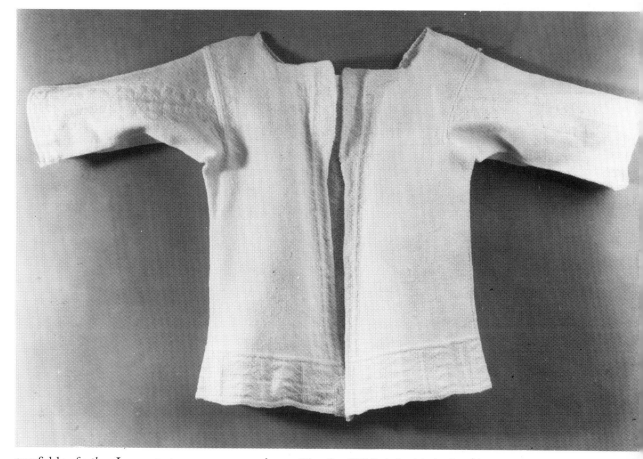

twofold: *firstly*, I want to encourage the growing band of skilled machine-knitters to try dressmaking and tailoring with some of the beautiful fabrics which they can produce at home at a fraction of the normal price. (If *your* dressmaking experience is limited, it is well worth going to an Adult Education class to learn more.) *Secondly*, those who, like me, are already addicted dressmakers, should be learning how to knit their own fabrics. Go into almost any ready-to-wear shop and you will find that a high proportion of the stock consists of cut-and-sew garments: T-shirts, track suits, pullovers, dresses, suits, jackets, coats etc., all made from knitted fabrics in a wide variety of weights and textures, by dress-making and tailoring methods. So, why not do it yourself, save money and be superbly well dressed into the bargain?

Fig. 3 *Child's knitted jacket in white cotton—seventeenth-/eighteenth-century (Victoria and Albert Museum, Crown Copyright)*

KEY to diagrams and abbreviations

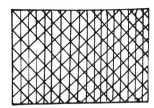

Knit—R.S.

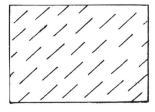

Woven fabric—R.S.

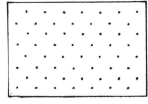

Interfacing

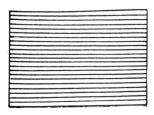

Knit—W.S.

Woven fabric—W.S.

C.B.	Centre Back
C.F.	Centre Front
R.S.	Right Side
W.S.	Wrong Side
s.a.	seam allowance
st. stit.	straight stitch
tog.	together
ZZ	zigzag

Woven fabric
Where this term is used in the text, it refers to weft-and-warp woven fabric, produced in a textile factory, e.g. velvet, cotton poplin, polyester lining, etc. Where I have intended to indicate that a woven fabric has been made on a domestic knitting machine, I have used the terms *knitweave* or *knitwoven*.

Note Specific numbers of dressmaking patterns are not included because delay between preparation and publication inevitably means that many will no longer be available.

1 Equipment for cut-and-sew

The equipment needed for cut-and-sew is roughly the same as that needed for general dressmaking. (List of manufacturers and stockists on pp. 113–6.)

FOR PRESSING
A steam iron
This is essential for the initial process of pressing the fabric before cutting, as well as for pressing needed at various stages in making up. If you are considering buying a new one, look for the following points:

1 It should be designed to be filled with *tap* water rather than distilled water.
2 The sole should have *plenty* of steam escape holes, not just a few in the middle.
3 It should be comfortable to use and not too heavy.
4 Many of the newer irons can produce an extra shot of steam and/or a fine spray of water at the touch of a button. Both these extras can be very useful.
5 If you are left-handed, make sure that the cable can be transferred to the other side of the heel, or that it is situated centrally so that the iron can be used by either hand.

A Teflon iron pad
This eliminates the need for a pressing cloth because it prevents the iron from making a shine on the fabric. It is particularly useful for knitted fabrics, especially acrylics, and is simply a cover which fits over the sole-plate of the iron, held in place by a metal spring band. One version of this is the Easyway, obtainable from demonstrators operating in the larger department stores.

Clean-Iron
This is a chemical cleaner for iron sole-plates, manufactured by Vilene, in stick form, enclosed in a plastic case. Follow their instructions carefully. Obtainable from haberdashers who stock other Vilene products.

Ironing board
This should stand firmly and be slightly padded. If you have a choice, buy the largest one you can afford and have room for. Cover it firmly with old sheeting or one of the milium covers now on sale.

Sleeve board
Also padded and covered.

A seam roller
This is used for pressing seams and avoiding the chance of getting an imprint of the edges of the seam allowances on the right side of the fabric. It can be made from an old wooden pastry roller minus its handles; alternatively buy a 30cm (12in.) length of dowelling from a builder's merchant. Cover either of these with a layer of blanket cloth and a layer of cotton sheeting, sewn tightly in place.

A pounding block
This is used for pounding bulky edges immediately after steam pressing, to obtain a sharp edge. You can buy the real thing

from a large haberdashery store, but they tend to be expensive. Again, a builder's merchant can supply a very adequate substitute in the form of 30cm (12in.) of wooden banister rail. The wood should be left totally untreated as it has to absorb steam.

A tailor's ham

Use this for pressing curved seams or for moulding a collar, where the ironing board or sleeve board is too flat. It consists of a ham-shaped (or it can be oval) bag of strong, closely-woven fabric, stuffed with sawdust. When making the bag, cut four identical shapes, approximately 40cm (16in.) long and 25cm (10in.) across the widest part. Two of these should be cut from strong calico, the third from a closely woven wool cloth, such as flannel, and the fourth from a strong woven cotton, such as sheeting. Put the four pieces together in the following order: calico, wool, cotton, calico. Seam all round by machine, using a small stitch length and leaving a gap for turning. Turn so that on the outside you have cotton on one half and wool on the other. Stuff *really tightly* with clean, dry sawdust; when no more can possibly be put in, sew up the gap.

A small pressing mitt

As the name suggests, this is a kind of padded bag which fits over the hand (or over the end of the sleeve board) and is of great value for pressing small curved areas, such as the top of a sleeve. It can be home-made or purchased from a haberdasher quite reasonably.

A thick Turkish towel

Spread this over the ironing board when pressing a heavily textured fabric which you do not wish to flatten completely.

A thin linen or fine wool pressing cloth

FOR PATTERN CUTTING (if you wish to try cutting your own)

Metric squared pattern paper

Small packets can be bought from haberdashers. If you are going to use very much, it is cheaper by the quire (25 sheets) from a wholesaler.

Coloured ball-point or felt-tipped pens

Metric/imperial long ruler

FOR ALTERING COMMERCIAL PATTERNS
Coloured felt-tip or ball-point pens

Spare transparent paper

Greaseproof works well.

Rulers

A 30cm (12in.) ruler marked in inches and centimetres. A metre ruler can be bought inexpensively in wallpaper shops, but check that it really is straight.

FOR MEASURING (all obtainable from good haberdashery departments)

Rulers

As above.

A fibreglass tape measure

This should preferably have inches and centimetres on both sides and measure exactly 1.5cm wide. This is a very useful guide for estimating the standard s.a.

A 15cm (6in.) metal measure with a sliding marker

This is useful for checking the depth of a waistband or of a hem.

A skirt hem-marker

This is a wooden ruler fixed vertically in a metal tripod stand, with a metal adjustable fitment which makes it easy for someone else to insert pins in the skirt, at a level distance from the ground, all the way round. This is essential for achieving a really level hem. Husbands and children can soon be taught to use this!

FOR PINNING

Glass (or plastic) headed pins

These are made of fine steel. The ordinary ones get lost, either in the knitting or on the floor, and so it is well worth paying a little more for these. It is also worth having a few extra-long pins, also with glass heads. These are necessary sometimes for extra bulky knitting. It is possible to buy ball-pointed pins but personally I have not found these to be really necessary.

FOR CUTTING

A large, steady table

Mine is also our breakfast table, and it is covered with a vinyl-coated cotton cloth printed in large symmetrical squares. This is amazingly helpful when checking that the grain of the fabric is straight before cutting, for cutting bias strips, etc.

A pair of bent-handle shears

This should measure 18–20cm in length (7–8in.). The weight is up to you but, on the whole, lightweight ones are less tiring. Some knits can be tough to cut. Keep your cutting-out shears really sharp and never let anyone use them for paper cutting, which blunts them.

Scissors

Choose a pair of small sewing scissors with one blunt end to avoid snagging when trimming. Keep very sharp. It is also useful to have a pair of serrated-edge scissors, although these are an optional extra. They are more effective sometimes for cutting knits, especially when the fibre is synthetic.

A seam ripper

Not for actually ripping seams but for the otherwise tedious job of unpicking stitches. These generally come in two sizes and I find the smaller one more useful. Use them, too, for cutting the slit in a machine-stitched buttonhole, cutting from the end towards the centre. After a certain amount of use they do become blunt and need to be replaced.

FOR MARKING (i.e. transferring pattern symbols from the pattern to the fabric)

Tailor's chalk

This is useful for making a mark which does not need to be too precise and is not going to be needed for very long. It tends to rub off rather easily.

A Pikaby marking pen

This looks and works like an ordinary fibre-tip pen but the ink in it is immediately removable by applying water. (Even a licked finger will do it!) At present it comes only in turquoise blue. Marking with this pen can be absolutely precise so this is a very valuable aid.

Chalk pencils

These are obtainable in haberdashery departments. They produce a more precise mark and one which is less likely to rub off than one made with tailor's chalk. As these are usually made in pale colours, they are good for marking dark fabrics where the Pikaby pen would not show up.

Coloured pencils

These are for marking turquoise blue knitting or any other colour which cannot be successfully marked by the Pikaby pen. Dipping the point in a cup of water helps to transfer the colour. It is worthwhile doing a test to make sure that the mark will wash out, before marking any part of the garment which is likely to show. Do not use felt-tip pens or anything containing ink.

Small adhesive paper labels

These can be bought in packets from the stationer's shop, and are very useful for sticking temporarily to your garment pieces to indicate 'right side', 'left side', 'wrong side of the fabric' etc.

Note Thread marking can be used, but the traditional tailor's tacks tend to fall out and, in some cases, to be insufficiently accurate.

FOR SEWING
A swing-needle sewing machine
This is a machine in which the needle is able to move, if desired, from side to side, as well as backwards and forwards. This enables you to do ZZ stitching and, consequently, buttonholes and various over-edge stitches. (See Chapter 3 on how to choose and use sewing machines.)

An overlocking machine
This is an optional extra, but for cut-and-sew work the advantages of having one are tremendous. They can simply trim and oversew seam edges or they can make a chain-stitch seam as well, all in one operation. The technique is slightly different from using an ordinary sewing machine, but there are now a number of new domestic versions coming on to the market and they are surprisingly easy to learn to use. You would need to use it in conjunction with your sewing machine, not in place of it. It is the perfect answer to the problem of sewing really neat, flat seams in knitwear. (See Chapter 3 for how to buy and use.)

Threads
For cut-and-sew work, your threads must always be made from *polyester*, not pure cotton. This is because the thread must have some elasticity in order to allow the seam to stretch a certain amount. Polyester has this necessary stretchability; cotton will break when stretched. You can also use the newer threads which consist of a polyester core wrapped with cotton. If you are using an overlocker, you will need to buy your thread on large reels, preferably of 1,000m. These are also more economical for use on your sewing machine. Keep a range of large reels in basic colours for most of your machining, and then you will only need to buy the odd small one when it is essential to have a perfect colour match. Invisible nylon thread can be useful, particularly for attaching gold or silver trimmings—but it is difficult to avoid having tiny ends project-ing on the inside, which can irritate the skin. 'Bulked' nylon (soft and fluffy) is available for use on overlockers.

Bobbins
Keep a good supply of bobbins so that you do not have to unwind one to put on another colour. Make sure that they are the right type for your machine. Ideally, have a special bobbin box, obtainable from haberdashery stores, to prevent them from tangling.

A lint brush
This removes dust from under the feed teeth, around the bobbin race, etc.

Oil
This must be special sewing machine oil. Some modern machines do not need oiling: consult your instruction book.

Sewing machine needles
Never carry on sewing with a bent or blunt needle. You could be damaging your fabric and also your machine. Consult your machine instruction book to make sure you are buying the right range of needles for knitted fabrics; these are usually labelled *ballpoint*—they have rounded points which slide more easily between threads instead of piercing them. There are others labelled *stretch*, which are the same as ballpoints except that they are made of a different material to counteract static: use them in cases where synthetic fibres appear to be the cause of skipped stitches. Use the usual pointed needles when sewing woven fabrics.

Needle sizes
There are two scales. The British/American scale runs from 9 (the finest) to 18 (the thickest). Continental sizing runs from 60 (finest) to 110 (thickest). For most machining on knitted fabrics, you will require a size in about the middle of these ranges, i.e. 14 or 80, but be prepared to go up or down a size as necessary. Also, use a finer needle

when sewing lining fabrics, which are
usually quite thin.

A good light
Have one poised over the sewing end of
your machine, in addition to the light
already attached to the machine. The
Anglepoise type of lamp is ideal. Never try
to sew in a bad light.

A comfortable seat
This should be high enough for you to be
able to look down on the needle end of your
machine.

FOR FITTING
A long mirror
Try on your garment at frequent intervals
and check on the fit and the appearance.

A piece of tape
Have a piece long enough to tie around the
waist to establish and mark the waistline on
skirts, dresses, trousers etc.

A hand mirror
Use this to see your back view in the long
mirror.

2 Notions and their use

The word *notions* is found on the packet backs of most of the dressmaking patterns on sale in this country. It is the American term which covers all the items of haberdashery necessary for the completion of the particular garment illustrated on the front of the packet. The following list covers most of the notions which I have found appropriate for cut-and-sew. For manufacturers and suppliers of some items, see pp. 113–7.

INTERFACINGS

These are the stabilising fabrics which are used between the garment fabric layers, on large or small areas, to give stability to the main fabric and to keep the garment edges firm. Sometimes only the facings are interfaced, but if your knitted fabric is very unstable, it is quite possible to interface whole pieces of it before cutting. (See Chapter 6 on how to use interfacings.) The following are especially recommended for cut-and-sew work: all are fusible, i.e. they can be ironed on to the wrong side of the knitted fabric where they will stick.

Fusible knitted nylon jersey. (Easy-knit in U.S.A.)

Vilene Supershape Iron-on in a choice of three weights: light (comes in white and charcoal), medium and heavy (both in white only). (Pellon in U.S.A.)

Fusible woven cotton muslin This can be used in small areas, such as collars, wherever stretching needs to be completely eliminated. (Shapewell in U.S.A.)

Vilene Fold-a-Band This is a double strip, 3cm (approx. $1\frac{1}{4}$in.) wide, of iron-on interfacing. The lightweight one is very useful for making absolutely straight front bands, cuffs, pocket tops etc. It is also recommended for keeping pleats in place, but this would probably not be of much value to machine knitters who are able to achieve permanent pleating on their knitting machines. The heavier weight is very good for interfacing waistbands, making them resistant to rolling and stretching.

Sew-in interfacings are very rarely necessary in my experience and, in fact, actually create problems in cut-and-sew work.

LININGS
Lining fabrics

For lining skirts, jackets, coats etc. You can eliminate the stretch factor in a jacket and help to limit it in a skirt, by using a woven polyester, for example. If some stretch is required, consider the antistatic nylon jersey available from some drapers' shops. Linings labelled 'antistatic' will avoid the problem of clinging either to the main fabric or to your tights or stockings. Lining fabric should be slippery in texture and must be compatible with the main fabric. For lining transparent fabrics, try using a flesh colour to eliminate differences between lined and unlined parts of the garment.

Use lining fabric also for making facings; for example, for the neck and armholes of a sleeveless dress which has no other lining. The woven lining fabric, having no stretch quality, stabilises these edges very efficiently. A light interfacing fused to the facings is usually advisable.

Jackets and coats can be lined with fur

Fig. 4 *Pure wool-knit jacket, lined with fur fabric and zipped (a close-up of colour photograph opp. p. 73)*

fabric, which also stabilises the knitting (see fig. 4). I have made a zipped blouson jacket in knit lined with a firm showerproof polyester cotton, which then became reversible! Printed silk makes a very luxurious lining for a coat or jacket, particularly if it matches the blouse underneath. A knitted-fabric dressing gown becomes superbly warm if lined with purchased brushed nylon jersey. Make sure, however, that the two fabrics will hang together well.

Interlining fabrics

To add additional warmth in the form of an extra layer between fabric and lining. Use purchased knitted (or woven) domette or polyester wadding. Quilting can be done through the fabric and the interlining together, if required.

Underlining fabrics

Used for mounting thin, loosely con-structed, unstable or transparent fabrics such as knitted lace (p. 88). Use a closely woven fabric, similar in weight to the main fabric. The degree of stiffness in the under-lining fabric will depend on the style of the garment.

FASTENERS
Buttons

The choice of these is endless, but *very* important to the look of the finished garment. Cheap, ill-chosen buttons can ruin the effect, but the right ones can lift an otherwise simple garment into the couture class. It really is worth spending, perhaps, more time and cash than you would nor-mally think necessary, to find just the right ones. Wooden and horn buttons look parti-cularly good on knits, as do ceramics, pro-viding they are not too heavy. Try small antique shops for Victorian, Edwardian, Art Noveau, or 'thirties geometric buttons; also look for smoked pearl, which has an uncanny knack of going with almost every-thing.

If you are combining a woven fabric with your knit, try having professionally covered buttons made in the woven fabric. Your knit can also be used for this, pro-viding it is not too loose in texture. (Interlining may be necessary.) Harlequin do this at a very reasonable cost and practi-cally always by return of post (p. 113).

Zips

I find that the lightweight nylon or poly-ester zips are best for cut-and-sew work. They are far stronger than they look and, properly inserted, they scarcely ever break. They are also far easier to sew in than the heavier metal kind. Choose the type with the smallest, flattest pull-tag.

If the zip is to be the focal point of a garment, such as down the front of a blouson jacket, try to find the big, chunky, moulded nylon ones which are open-ended. Large haberdashery departments have them in a variety of colours.

Corset hooks and eyes

These come in black or silver and are excellent for holding the *inside* end of a skirt waistband. Being very strong, they take the strain well, so that the outer lap of the waistband can then be held down by small hooks and buttonholed loops, with no danger of the loops breaking. They are available from haberdashers.

Small hooks and bars (not eyes)

Also in black or silver, these are good for the outer lap of skirt waistbands or for back neck fastenings etc.

Fig. 5 *Non-sew snap fasteners (a close-up of garment shown in colour photograph opp. p. 96)*

Non-sew snap fasteners

These are now available in a variety of types for different weights of fabric. This is one way of giving a highly professional look to a simple garment. The 'Poppa' range by Newey Goodman are particularly good. The pincer type of applicator (which usually requires considerable strength to manipulate efficiently) has been replaced by a folding plastic applicator which is used with a hammer and a wooden block. You will, initially, need to purchase this tool for inserting them. It is advisable to make the band (into which these fasteners will go) of a firm, woven fabric, or of knit faced with woven fabric. Do not try to put them into the knit fabric alone. They are very effective and surprisingly strong (see fig. 5).

Velcro nylon tape

One strip, with hooked nap, fastens firmly to the other strip, which has a looped nap. This resists pulling yet will actually peel apart quite easily. Useful, instead of zips or buttons, to enable small children or handicapped people to cope with their own fastenings. Also for rainproof clothing. It comes in 1.5cm and 2cm widths (approximately $\frac{5}{8}$in. and $\frac{3}{4}$in.) in a selection of colours. When cut, it does not fray and is very easy to machine on to any flat, straight fabric.

BELTS

Here again, it is worth spending extra time, trouble and perhaps cash. However, most of the real leather treasures in my own collection of belts have come from local bring-and-buys and even jumble sales.

Harlequin also make very presentable belts from your own fabric, knitted or woven.

Study the craft books and magazines for various ways of making your own belts in macrame, leather, embroidered canvas etc., and fasten these with unusual or antique buckles. There are some beautiful old enamel ones around, which need only good quality matching ribbon to make the belt part, possibly stiffened with petersham. Then use the same ribbon for covered buttons or for binding the edges of your knit garment.

Avoid the tie belts, which tend to look like the old gym-tunic girdles. They do not flatter any figure! Try cummerbunds instead, as illustrated in photograph opp. p. 96.

TAPES, ELASTICS AND BONDING MATERIALS

Tape

For staying seams which must not stretch. Cotton tape, approximately 0.6cm ($\frac{1}{4}$in.) wide. See Chapter 6 for use.

Stretch lace

For machining over, and so covering, the raw edge of a hem. This, after blind-hemming, will stretch with the rest of the garment (see fig. 6). Shopkeepers tend to claim ignorance of stretch lace. Market haberdashery stalls are a more likely source as they often buy up stock from the manu-

Fig. 6 *Stretch lace machined over raw edge of hem*

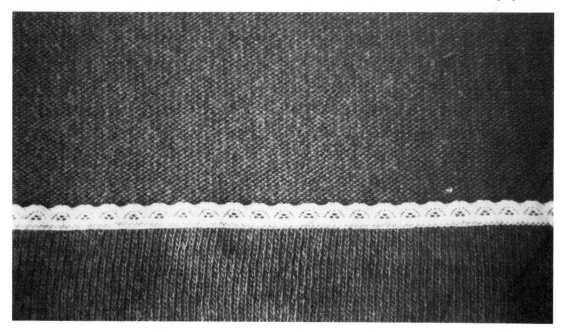

facturers of corsetry. Try to collect a stock of various colours by buying some whenever you find it. The width should be between 1.3cm (½in.) and 2.5cm (1in.). The edges should be reasonably straight.

Skirt-petersham

For skirt tops where an ordinary waistband is not required. It should be made of polyester or nylon, rather than cotton, for strength and stability. It can be straight or curved.

Petersham ribbon

This is the millinery type, which is thinner and softer than skirt-petersham. Very useful for facing the straight front edges of an unlined knitted jacket or cardigan, and this will then take machined buttonholes very well (see figs. 7(a) and (b)).

Elastics

For defining the waist of a dress or for the top of a skirt, and many other uses. Choose a good quality one in a suitable width. Make sure that it will not roll over and so become narrower than you intend. Woven elastics curl less than braided elastics. There is a type which can be used like petersham inside the top of a skirt, in place of a waistband, allowing comfortably for expansion of the waist.

Vilene Bondaweb

For fusing pieces of contrasting fabric to the main fabric for appliqué work. Add your own initials, motifs, flowers cut from chintz. Imagine a dress in a feather-pattern print, with its toning knitted jacket appliquéd with one or two of the feathers. The possibilities are endless.

Fig. 7a *Edge of knit (R.S.) faced with ribbon and buttonholed*

Fig. 7b *Edge of knit (W.S.) faced with ribbon and buttonholed*

Vilene Wundatrim
This fairly recent addition to the range consists of a continuous strip of bonding medium in three different widths: 7mm, 1.5cm and 2.3cm (approx. $\frac{1}{4}$in., $\frac{5}{8}$in. and 1in.). I find it very useful indeed for fixing braid, tape, ribbon etc. in position, with the touch of an iron, before machine stitching.

Note For best results with all Vilene products, follow their printed instructions to the letter.

TRIMMINGS
There is such an infinite variety available that I could go on for ever. Simply use your imagination, or, if you are not very imaginative, look for ideas in the windows of some of the more exclusive shops. I am still trying to find the time to try out a version of a simple cream-coloured two-piece I once saw. The hem of the skirt, the edge of the collar and the sleeve ends were bordered with three bands of very narrow satin ribbon in ivory, deep cream and coffee, simply machined on flat, straight and quite close together: so simple and yet so effective.

Beware of mixing different trimmings too much, unless you want an ethnic effect, and do not overtrim. Also, practise the methods of application before starting on the actual garment. Pin everything on first and check that you really like the effect, before stitching. Check that the trimming and the garment fabric can be cleaned or laundered in the same way.

Here are a few suggestions:

Woven braids
These will bend easily around curved edges. These can be purchased or made up on your knitting machine.

Fold-over braid
Sold by the metre by haberdashers, either flat and about 3cm (1$\frac{1}{4}$in.) wide, or already pressed in half lengthwise. This is also good for binding curves (see fig. 8). It can be

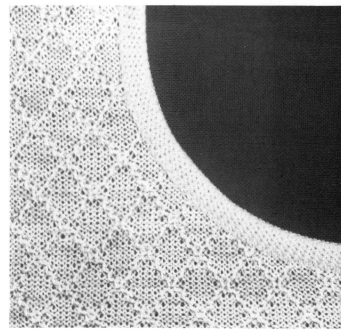

Fig. 8 *Fold-over braid sewn to a curved edge*

made of wool, silk, rayon, nylon or acrylic, so try to match it up with the fibre content of your knitting yarn, to avoid cleaning or laundering problems.

Piping cord
This comes in various thicknesses, so choose the one suitable for the thickness of your knit. Use for giving an extra finishing touch to collar and cuff edges or to define the seaming (see fig. 9). Cut the bias strips for covering the cord from a lightweight woven fabric, such as polyester/cotton, or from satin for a shiny look.

Ribbons
Choose from silk, polyester, nylon or cotton; plain or satin; velvet; metallic; embroidered etc.; all come in various widths. They can be used as a matching colour, a toning shade of the same colour or a complete contrast. All can be used for trimming, in straight lines with mitred corners. Curves are difficult and would probably not look good. Consider also the printed cotton border strips which are

Fig. 9 *Dress in bright courtelle-knit, well-pressed;
seams piped and neck faced with poly/linen woven
fabric (a close-up of colour photograph opp. p. 96)*

22

available from interior decorating or soft furnishing suppliers. Laura Ashley make some very pretty ones.

Lace

This can be most attractive when combined with knitted fabrics. Obviously use a thicker, more chunky lace with a thicker knit. Try a lace ruffle at neck and cuffs, or flat strips over the knit in bands. Lace can also be effectively cut to shape and used for a yoke or front neck inset.

Broderie anglaise

I would suggest you use this only with cotton knits because of laundry problems.

Ricrac

Applied flat, or put into a seam so that only half of its width shows as a line of tiny half-circles, this can define a focal seam in the same way as piping (see fig. 10).

Fig. 10 *Ricrac braid sewn into a seam which is then top-stitched on the R.S. through all thicknesses*

Fur trimming

Real or synthetic, this can be bought by the metre and sewn on. In the case of real fur, check that the weight of the fur is not too much for the strength of the fabric.

Beading

This can be purchased in strip form and sewn on, usually by hand. Alternatively, use separate beads as a form of embroidery or to form lines or edgings, also to be sewn on by hand.

Cuff-ribbing

For use in cuffs, collars and waistbands. This can, of course, be made on your knitting machine, incorporating elastic. Alternatively, you can buy it from some drapers in various colours, either flat (by the metre) or tubular (in packets) (see fig. 11).

Fig. 11 *Cuff made from purchased flat ribbing, sewn to bouclé-knit trouser leg (a close-up of garment shown in colour photograph opp. p. 73)*

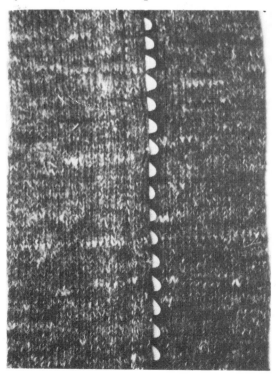

23

Knotted fringing
This can be made or purchased. The fibre content should match your knitting fibre.

Machine top-stitching
This is frequently the only trimming needed. It is done during the construction process, either in your normal polyester machining thread or in a thicker thread. Top-stitching thread, all polyester, is manufactured by the same firms who produce the polyester, or cotton-wrapped polyester, sewing threads. This thread is thicker, however. Alternatively, use Sylko 30, or two reels of Sylko 40 together.

3 Sewing machines and overlockers

YOUR SEWING MACHINE

This is the most important, and probably the most expensive, item on your list of cut-and-sew equipment. The desired professional finish to your home-made clothes is obtained only when the machine is efficient and you, the operator, use that machine with understanding and confidence. The efficiency of the machine comes from good design and engineering, features which are not always available at the lower end of the market. Your own understanding and confidence will grow rapidly with practice, a little guidance from your sewing machine supplier and constant reference to the machine instruction book.

If your present machine is designed to do only straight stitching (i.e. the needle cannot swing from side to side), you will certainly be able to do some cut-and-sew work, but your scope will be somewhat limited because you will not be able to produce a seam which will stretch without snapping the stitches. You can stretch the fabric as you sew, but then it may not contract again, leaving you with a permanently stretched seam. (If you have already experienced this disaster, try running a thread of Shirlastic down the seamline with a needle, drawing it up until the seam has contracted to its original length; it will then look better and will still have the stretch quality.) A straight stitch machine is also unable to neaten seams effectively on the inside of the garment: some form of seam binding or total lining would therefore be necessary. In cases where a knitted fabric is being attached to a woven fabric (e.g. knitted sleeves in a tweed jacket) there would be no problem because the seam would be unable to stretch anyway.

If your machine has a basic ZZ stitch (without blind-hem, three-step ZZ etc.) then you can sew a seam which will have the necessary stretch quality; seam finishing, however, may still be a problem.

STITCHES

The following five utility stitches are the ones which are most useful for cut-and-sew work. Most modern swing-needle machines incorporate these.

Straight stitch (see fig. 12)

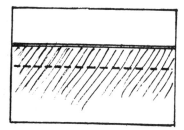

Fig. 12 *Straight stitch*

Use this for seams on woven fabrics, linings etc., on knit fabrics which have been stabilised, and for tailored, fully-lined garments. Also for decorative top-stitching and for quilting.

Zigzag (ZZ) stitch (see fig. 13)
Use this for seams in knitted fabrics where stretch is needed, usually using a stitch width of $\frac{1}{2}$ to $1\frac{1}{4}$. Use also for oversewing seam edges on woven fabrics, for buttonholes and for appliqué.

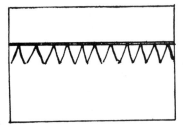

Fig. 13   *Zigzag stitch*

Serpentine, elastic or 3-step ZZ stitch (see fig. 14)
Use this for oversewing seam edges on loosely woven or knitted fabric and for sewing elastic to a fabric. It can be attractive when used for top-stitching and for machined hems which need to stretch.

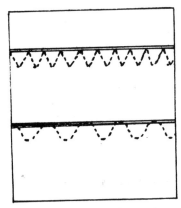

Fig. 14   *Serpentine, elastic or 3-step zigzag stitch*

Blind-hem or elastic-blind-hem stitch (see fig. 15)
Your machine may have one or both of these, with a special sewing foot for the purpose. The plain blind-hem can be used for knit fabrics, providing the tension is kept fairly slack to allow for stretching. Alternatively, stretch the knit fabric a little during the hemming process. The straight or small ZZ stitches are done on the hem edge and the needle moves to the left to catch in the fold of the garment at fixed intervals.

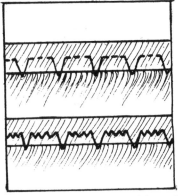

Fig. 15   *Blind-hem and elastic blind-hem stitches*

Overlock stitches (see fig. 16)
There are many different versions of this useful stitch, which, with the s.a. previously cut, with scissors, down to approximately 0.6cm ($\frac{1}{4}$in.), sews the seam and oversews the seam edges in one operation. Bernina make a special foot for knitted fabrics (No. 528) to use with this stitch which they call the Vari-overlock (see fig. 17). I find this excellent for seams in knitwear.

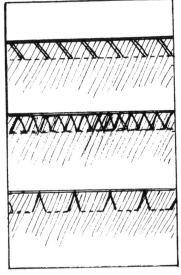

Fig. 16   *Overlock stitches*

Fig. 17a *Vari-overlock presser foot (Bernina)*

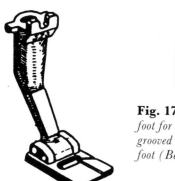

Fig. 17b *Special presser foot for knits, front view (Bernina)*

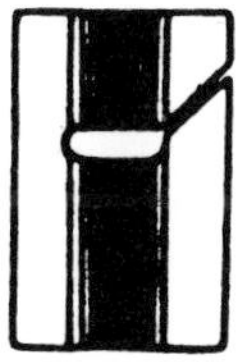

Fig. 17c *Special presser foot for knits, showing the grooved underside of the foot (Bernina)*

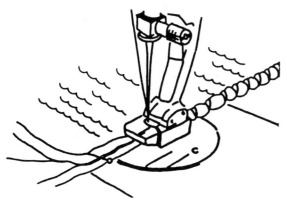

Fig. 17d *Sewing the Vari-overlock stitch with the special knit foot*

When considering buying a new machine, make sure that the overlock stitch can be executed with the bulk of the garment lying to the left of the machine, and not simply using the blind-hem stitch, with the bulk of the garment having to be pushed through the centre of the machine. Bernina now make a separate attachment (which can be added to most of their models) called Cut'n'Sew; this actually cuts the fabric edge and overlocks it at the same time. Many of the most recent machines to come on to the market incorporate this ability, to cut and overlock, into the machine itself as part of its range of capabilities. However, this type of overlocking should not be confused with that produced by a purpose-built overlocking machine which, having a very different system of stitching, produces an equally different result (pp. 34–8). Whilst these added or incorporated cut-and-overlock mechanisms on sewing machines are excellent for general dressmaking purposes, they are not ideal for most of the fabrics made on a domestic knitting machine. So far, I have found them unable to cope with more than fine, closely knitted fabrics, similar to those which can be purchased from a draper.

Ideally, have a sewing machine which will do the previously listed five utility stitches really well on all fabrics, and save up for a separate domestic overlocker if you do not already possess one.

Triple-straight and triple-ZZ stitches
These are useful for sewing a seam which is required to cope with a great deal of pulling and stretching, e.g. trouser crutch seams, armhole seams etc. The machine, roughly speaking, does two stitches forward and one back, thus covering each stitch space three times. There is one snag to this, however: it is practically impossible to unpick the stitching if you have made a mistake. Use it only when you are absolutely sure that the fitting is correct.

There are also a great many different

embroidery stitches available, plus, in some cases, the ability to programme a series of these and even to include mirror images. Whether or not you feel these are essential is something only you can decide. I have come across many machines which have apparently been able to do 99 different embroidery stitches but which also have had tedious tension problems and a complete inability to produce a good buttonhole.

BUYING A MACHINE

If you are buying a new machine you will need to do some careful research. The development of microprocessors has enabled the newest machines to incorporate a vast range of both utility and embroidery stitches, all simply operated at the touch of a button. At first sight, these are somewhat daunting but they are, in fact, easier for a beginner to use than many of the older machines, just because the programming is so comprehensive. Decisions with regard to needle position, stitch length, thread tension, foot pressure etc. are made automatically by the machine, and needle size and choice of sewing foot are clearly indicated, leaving less room for error on the part of the operator.

1 If you have no special need for the extra embroidery stitches, look for a good quality machine which will perform the five utility stitches really well, especially on knitted fabrics. Before buying, try out all these stitches, including the buttonhole, yourself. Use a variety of fabrics, including knits, for your test sewing, not just the calico which the shop demonstrator may be using.

2 Buy a free-arm rather than a flat-bed machine. This means that the stitching part of the machine is on a separate arm, well above the machine base, so that it is possible to slip an armhole or a neck opening right around the arm, thus making the sewing area more accessible. All free-arm machines have some means of extending the arm into the equivalent of a flat-bed,

usually by the addition of a table which slides on to surround it.

3 Buy only from a reputable sewing machine shop where the owner is a registered agent for several different makes of machine including the leading European ones, i.e. Bernina from Switzerland, Husqvarna (Viking) from Sweden, Pfaff from Germany and Elna from Switzerland. (For patriots, I regret that at the time of writing there is no sewing machine made in Great Britain.) Amongst the Japanese machines, look for Frister + Rossmann, Riccar and Toyota.

4 Make sure that you will get after-sales service and tuition. You should be able to go back to the dealer for a lesson or two after you have had the machine at home for a while and have become accustomed to it. By that time you will have a much clearer idea of what questions you really need to ask.

5 Be prepared to spend time trying out various machines. In fact, the whole business is rather like buying a car: you need to find the one that suits you, is within your budget, will do what you require of it and will run with the minimum of problems.

6 Check on how easy it is to:
alter the tension on both needle and bobbin threads,
change the stitch length and stitch width,
change the feet,
change the needle,
remove the bobbin,
wind the bobbin,
thread the machine from thread winder spindle to needle, and
open up various parts of the machine for oiling and cleaning.

Check also on whether the shuttle can be removed easily so that, if you do get a tangle in the shuttle race, it can be swiftly cleared.

7 Try stitching very slowly to make sure that you will be able to control the speed.

There is nothing worse than a machine which tends to run away with the operator. Many machines now have a maximum/minimum speed control switch. They may also have an electronic foot control. This means that a special electrical circuit controls the speed of the motor but gives the needle the full power of penetration, enabling the operator to sew thick layers of fabric slowly and carefully when necessary.

8 Look at the instruction book which goes with the machine. Make sure that it is easy to understand, with clear diagrams and specific instructions. Sometimes they consist of rather dubious translations from a foreign language with a lot of room for mis-understanding.

9 Make sure that you can carry the machine reasonably easily, unless it is always going to remain in one place, ready for use. If you are hardly every likely to want to move it, it might be worth enquiring if the same model comes any cheaper without a travelling case. (In this situation, a plastic cover is usually supplied or you could make a dust-cover for it.)

10 Make sure that your sewing machine dealer has good back-up from the manufacturer of the machine you are considering. He should be able to obtain spare parts easily and he and/or his staff should have had training from the manufacturer. Some machine manufacturers have centres in this country where a home-sewing adviser is employed to answer queries and to help solve problems by letter, telephone or personal visit. Bernina and Elna run classes at their London centres, and Toyota do the same at Bromley, Kent.

11 When you finally get your new machine home, sit down with the instruction book and go through it carefully from beginning to end, finding out the function of each knob, dial, screw and lever. If you find it difficult at first to remember which is which, label them with the little adhesive price labels which you can buy from stationery shops.

If your machine is secondhand and the original instruction book is missing, write to the manufacturer or their agent in this country, and ask for a copy, quoting your model number. If all else fails, take the machine along to a friendly sewing machine dealer and be prepared to write your own instruction notes under his tutelage.

Automatic buttonholing

This simply means that the machine will sew one side of the buttonhole and will then reverse direction to sew the other side, thus eliminating the need to turn the fabric round.

Semi-automatic buttonholing

This means that the satin-stitch travels only forwards and so it is necessary to turn the fabric around at the halfway stage.

Personally, I find it preferable to use the semi-automatic method (even when I have a machine which will do the full buttonhole automatically), for two reasons. Firstly, I like to keep a very sharp eye on the progress of the buttonhole and this is easier when stitching forwards; secondly, because the stitch length can, in certain conditions, vary a little when reversing.

Make sure that your machine accessory box contains a special foot for buttonholing. The normal sewing foot does not have the special grooves on the underside which enable you to keep the sides of the buttonhole straight. Many manufacturers now also include a roller foot and recommend this for use with knitted fabrics.

The piping foot

This deserves a special mention in this context. This is the foot used for machining a fabric-covered cord into the edges of a garment or into the seams. In the case of most machines, the zipper-foot is used for this purpose, meeting the necessity to sew very close to the cord. There are a few manufacturers (e.g. Bernina and Husqvarna) who make a special foot for piping which actually guides the cord into the right position under the foot, making the operation surprisingly simple and foolproof (see fig. 18). Piping is a current fashion feature and is extremely effective in cut-and-sew clothes (see fig. 9). It also has the advantage of stabilising the seams in which it is sewn.

Fig. 18a *Bernina piping foot, front view*

Fig. 18b *Bernina piping foot, showing groove on underside which fits over cord*

USING YOUR SEWING MACHINE

As Angela Thompson writes in her excellent and extremely comprehensive book, *The Complete Book of the Sewing Machine*: 'Machine sewing requires patience and a calm attitude'. It could not be put more succinctly. Admittedly, there are a few machines around which defy even the most experienced and understanding operators but, on the whole, most machining problems can be solved by making one or two quite small adjustments, either to the machine controls or to the methods of using the machine.

When something goes wrong with your machine, do *not* simply twiddle every knob and dial in sight, hoping that you might accidentally come upon the right combination, because that way lies disaster.

Instead, try to analyse what is wrong, then work out the cause and try appropriate remedies. The list on pp. 33–4 should help.

Prevention is better than cure, so look after your machine. Keep it clean and oiled; see your instruction book for this. (There are some machines which require little or no oiling.)

Keep it covered when not in use. If the carrying case is awkward to use, simply pop a large plastic carrier bag over the machine to keep off the dust.

Check the wiring from time to time for safety. If worn patches appear on the cable, have the cable renewed. Do not interfere with the motor, however, unless you are a qualified electrician.

Check the positions of the needle, stitch length, stitch width, thread tension control and pattern selector before you start to sew; this will avoid starting with an error.

Make sure that you are using the correct size of needle for the weight of the fabric you are using. A needle which is too fine will soon become blunt or will bend, or even snap. Too thick a needle will cause puckering and uneven stitching.

Needle sizing	**Fine**	**Medium**		**Heavy**	
Continental	70	80	90	100	110
British and American	9	11	14	16	18

Use synthetic threads. Cotton thread simply does not have the necessary elasticity. Use a thread which is either 100 per cent polyester or one which is composed of a polyester core wrapped with cotton. Read the labels to make sure you are buying the right thread because there are a number of different manufacturers producing these now, as well as other types of thread. For example, the Swedish firm of Molnlycke does not, at present, make a cotton-wrapped polyester thread, but it does make a pure polyester machine thread, a machine embroidery thread, a pure cotton machine thread and a thicker thread in pure polyester for buttonholing and top-stitching. All look rather similar and are only distinguishable by the different spool colours: the 100 per cent polyester is on grey spools, and the others are on green, yellow and black spools respectively.

When threading the machine, remember that the presser foot must be *up* to allow the top thread to be correctly positioned between the tension plates. When the presser foot is lowered, the tension plates are closed tightly together. *Check* that you are using the correct presser foot for the job.

When starting to sew, make sure that the take-up lever is at its highest position and that both the needle thread and the bobbin thread are positioned under the presser foot and then drawn out together, over the back of the machine bed. Hold these two thread ends whilst sewing the first two or three stitches.

Do not start sewing right at the outer edge of the fabric, because it could get pushed down through the needle hole and result in a tangle. Instead, start stitching about 1cm ($\frac{3}{8}$in.) in from the end; after two or three stitches, reverse back to the end and then continue forward.

Avoid hitting pins or metal zip parts etc. If this does happen, you will have to renew the needle, as it will undoubtedly have been blunted or even bent.

Remember that different fabrics can produce quite different qualities of stitching. Always experiment first with spare pieces of your fabric so that you can adjust the tension, stitch length or whatever else seems to be necessary, before starting on the garment.

Test sewing for tension, pressure and balance

This procedure should be carried out whenever you start to sew a new fabric.

1 Cut two identical strips of the chosen fabric, about 20cm (8in.) long. Pin them together, placing the pins across the seam-line.

2 Make sure that the machine needle is of the right type and size.

3 Thread the machine, using the same type of thread through the needle as on the bobbin, but use contrasting colours which will show up well on the fabric, e.g. red needle thread and blue bobbin thread on white fabric.

4 Set the stitch length to 2–3, depending on fabric weight.

5 Make a line of stitching approximately 1.5cm ($\frac{5}{8}$in.) from, and parallel with, the long edges of the strip, from top to bottom.

6 Examine the stitching very carefully under a good light.

IF the top layer of fabric, despite pinning, gets pushed towards you as you sew, making it overlap the lower layer when you reach the end, then either the pressure on the presser foot is too heavy, or you need to use a roller foot for this particular fabric.

IF the fabric slips about, causing a wobbly stitching line, then the presser foot pressure is insufficient.

IF the seam is puckered, then either the top thread or the bobbin thread tensions (or possibly both) are too tight.

IF the stitching is looped on one side and tight on the other, then either the top thread tension or the bobbin thread tension is too loose.

IF the stitching line looks the same on both sides (i.e. you can see only red stitches on the top and blue stitches underneath) then you have correctly balanced stitching. But the seam could still be puckered, in which case both top and bottom tensions are too tight.

Remember that the machine has been adjusted, in the factory or in the retailer's shop, to give a good stitch on at least two layers of calico. You may well find the tension too tight when you need to sew one layer of fine lining fabric. It may be that some of the newest machines really do have effective self-adjusting tension controls, but always experiment to make sure when using thin fabrics.

Adjustments

The presser foot

The means of altering the pressure is usually one of the following:

1 a thumbscrew on top of the left-hand end of the machine, directly above the needle. Turning it clockwise increases the pressure and anticlockwise decreases the pressure;

2 a dial inside the lefthand end of the machine. Turning to a higher number increases pressure and to a lower number decreases the pressure, or

3 a press-down knob within a spring-release circle, on the left-hand end of the machine. Pressing down the knob increases pressure. Pressing the circle releases pressure.

The needle thread tension

The tension on the top thread is regulated by the tension dial. This is usually situated near the top left-hand side of your machine, where the thread is passed between two metal discs. The dial is usually numbered, except on very old straight-stitch machines. Berninas have a wheel on top of the machine and the tension is indicated by a plus/minus sign in a window in the front. Bringing up more of the *plus* side gives *more* tension. Conversely, more of the *minus* side gives *less* tension.

Where there are numbers, lower numbers indicate less tension; higher numbers indicate more tension.

Where there is a dial, turning the dial clockwise increases tension; turning the dial anticlockwise decreases tension.

Always try to get the tension right by adjusting the top thread tension first.

The bobbin thread tension

It may occasionally be necessary to adjust the tension on the bobbin thread.

To do this, locate the very small screw in the centre of the steel band which encircles the bobbin case or shuttle. Clockwise rotation of this screw tightens the band and anticlockwise rotation loosens it. Make only a very small adjustment before testing again: the equivalent of turning the hands of a clock by five or ten minutes.

You can get a fair idea of whether or not the bobbin tension is correct by suspending the bobbin, in its bobbin case, by the loose end of thread coming from the bobbin. If it drops immediately, the tension is too loose. If it will not drop at all when shaken quite hard, the tension is too tight. It should gradually drop when shaken gently. Bernina recommend doing this but with the bobbin case inside the shuttle and therefore weighed down by it (see fig. 19).

Fig. 19 *Testing the tension on the bobbin thread (Bernina)*

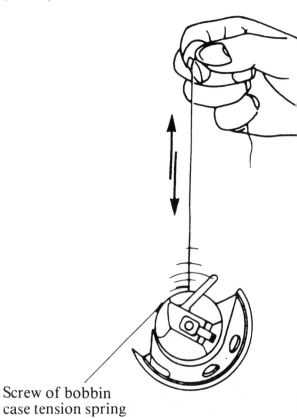

Screw of bobbin
case tension spring

Checklist for solving machine stitching problems

Problem		Possible cause
Needle thread breaks	**1**	Machine wrongly threaded
	2	Needle or thread too fine for fabric
	3	Needle wrongly inserted
	4	Needle bent
	5	Top tension too tight
	6	Blunt needle
	7	Rough edge in needle eye or throat plate
	8	Thread caught up in notch in spool
	9	A knot in the thread
Bobbin thread breaks	**1**	Lower tension too tight
	2	Bobbin overwound and sticking
	3	Lint or thread ends around bobbin case
	4	Rough edge on bobbin case
	5	Knot in bobbin thread
Uneven or skipped stitches	**1**	Jerky pressure on the foot control
	2	Wrong size or type of needle for thread or fabric
	3	Insufficient pressure on presser foot
	4	Anxious operator pulling fabric
	5	Machine wrongly threaded, top or bottom
	6	Bobbin unevenly wound
	7	The timing may need adjustment; consult an expert
Stitches not forming at all	**1**	Incorrect threading
	2	Bobbin empty
	3	Bent or blunt needle
	4	Needle incorrectly inserted
	5	Wrong type of needle
Puckered fabric	**1**	Either one or both tensions too tight
	2	Thread and/or needle wrong for fabric
	3	Too much pressure on presser foot
Needle breaks	**1**	Wrong needle for machine
	2	Needle incorrectly inserted
	3	Bobbin incorrectly inserted
	4	Too light a needle for thickness of fabric
	5	Operator pulling the fabric through or holding it back
	6	Needle has hit a pin, zip, snap-fastener or the presser foot, if this has been wrongly set
	7	Machine set to ZZ with the st. stit. needle plate in position
Machine not feeding fabric through properly	**1**	Feed dog may be lowered
	2	Insufficient pressure on presser foot
	3	Shiny fabric (e.g. vinyl) not being gripped by the feed teeth
	4	Anxious operator holding fabric back
	5	Stitch length set at or near 0

Looped stitches	**1**	Incorrect threading
	2	Upper tension (possibly lower) too loose
	3	Presser foot not down properly
	4	Needle bent, blunt or wrongly inserted
	5	Needle and/or thread unsuitable for fabric
Machine seems stiff	**1**	Lack of oil
	2	Machine too cold
	3	The moving parts may be clogged up with felt, dust etc.
Machine is noisy	**1**	Lack of oil
	2	Damaged needle
	3	Excessive vibration. Try standing the machine on a rubber mat or a folded blanket
Light comes on but rest of machine is not working		Probably a motor failure. Seek professional help

If you have tried, with the help of this list, to diagnose the problem and have failed to cure it, then get professional advice from a qualified sewing machine expert. A part may be damaged or the timing may have gone wrong. For electrical faults (apart from loose wires in the mains plug—and only tackle these if you are quite sure you know how!) always seek professional help. Never tamper with the motor unless you happen to be an expert yourself.

OVERLOCKERS

Those who already possess a domestic overlocking machine know well what a wonderful, time-saving addition it is to their dressmaking equipment. For cut-and-sew work, the overlocker provides the ideal method of seaming and finishing in one operation. These machines are comparatively new on the domestic market, and are modified versions of the industrial overlockers which have been used for years for making cut-and-sew knitwear, as an alternative to the more expensive fully-fashioned type. The price is roughly equivalent to that of a good modern sewing machine, but saving up for one would be worthwhile, especially if you intend to make cut-and-sew clothes for sale, either commercially or for private clients. I have come to regard my own overlocker as an indispensable aid, not only for its time-saving potential but also for the truly professional finish it gives.

There are a number of domestic overlockers on the market at the time of writing, all of which are made in Japan. The original Babylock (Juki), which for many years was supplied to schools and colleges, was a fairly large affair, similar to those used by clothing manufacturers. More recently, a portable domestic version was produced and other Japanese companies have followed with similar small overlockers in rapid succession.

The Mammylock (Aisin), and the Kawasaki (distributed in the U.K. by the Bogod Machine Co. of Sweden) come in three- and four-thread models. The new Babylock (Juki) and the Homelock (Brother) come in two-, three- and four-thread models. Frister + Rossmann produce an exceptionally well-designed range of overlockers (two-, three- and four-thread) also made in Japan, but to British specification. I have used my Frister-Lock 4 very successfully for much of my cut-and-sew work as well as for general dressmaking, and can thoroughly recom-

Fig. 20 *Multi-purpose Frister-Lock 4: a 2-needle 4-thread overlocker which will also just chain-stitch or just overcast (Frister + Rossmann Sewing Machines)*

mend it. The newer Frister Knit-Lock 5 is designed especially for knitted fabrics and produces even better results (see figs. 20, 21 and 22). The four-thread Riccar-Lock is also good for knits. Husqvarna have recently introduced a four-thread model called Huskylock.

In general, the *two-thread* machines trim the edges of the fabric and overlock them; the *three-thread* machines trim and do a true overlock stitch; the *four-thread* machines trim, make a chain-stitch seam and overlock the edge, in combination or separately.

All these domestic machines incorporate a protected cutting-blade which does the trimming. Most use standard needles, and the newer models have colour-coded and simplified threading systems.

The ability of the four-thread machines, either to trim, sew a seam and overlock it in one operation, or to simply trim and overlock one fabric edge, makes them ideal for cut-and-sew work.

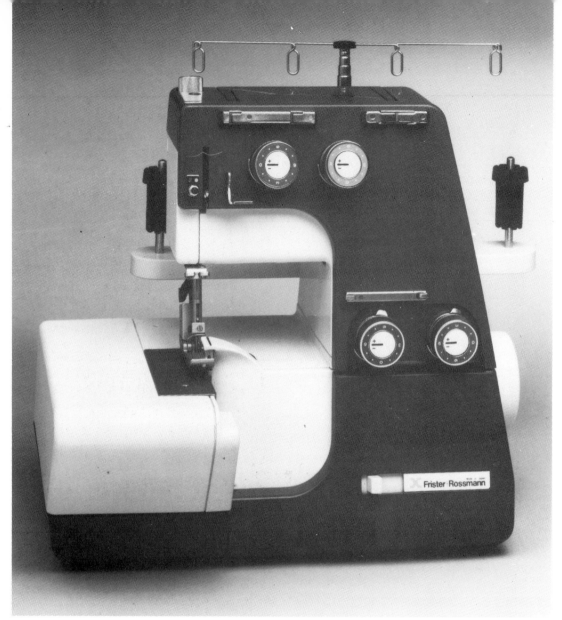

Fig. 21 *Frister-Knitlock 5: much more versatile and specially designed for knitted fabrics; 2 needles and 4 threads (Frister + Rossmann Sewing Machines)*

These overlockers do use up vast quantities of thread, but to my mind this is a small price to pay for the time they save and the neat finish they produce. Buy polyester thread for your overlocker in nothing less than 1,000m spools. A mail order firm (see address on p. 114) supplies these at reasonable cost. It is possible, too, to buy industrial thread in large cones at even cheaper rates. It is not always necessary, for this type of sewing, to use perfectly matching colours, so large reels in the basic shades of white, black, grey and beige would probably be adequate for most of your cut-and-sew projects.

Differences between sewing machines and overlockers

1 The overlocker has no bobbin. All the threads come from the top of the machine, and each has its own tension dial.

2 When the end of a seam is reached, the machine has to be kept running so that

Fig. 22 *Sample stitching on the Frister-Knitlock 5. From left to right: three and four thread overlocking on denim; three thread overlocking and corded overlocking on a fine knit, and overlocking on knitted fabric, using bulked nylon*

several inches of a chain are made by the threads. These ends are left projecting from the back of the foot, ready to start the next seam. (In practice, it speeds up the work if you feed seams under the foot, one after the other, snipping the thread chains between them afterwards.)

3 It is impossible to start sewing inside the edge of the fabric when using the cutter and overlocking mechanism. For example, when seaming, trimming and overlocking a circular armhole seam, the fabric has to be guided so that the stitching filters from the edge to the seamline at the start, and then filters off again at the end, the last few stitches having crossed the first ones.

It is possible, if your overlocker incorporates a chain-stitch seam mechanism, to sew the seam alone, inside the edge of the fabric. See your instruction book. The cutting knife is blocked by an additional needle-plate, and the overlocking needle does not operate.

Helpful hints on using your overlocking machine

1 Study the instruction book really carefully and get in plenty of practice before starting to sew a garment.

2 To begin with, thread the machine with a different colour for each tension dial, so that you will quickly be able to identify the function of each one. At this stage, it may be helpful to label each dial, 'chain-stitch looper', 'needle overlock', etc. This will also be helpful if you need to sort out tension problems.

3 Be very careful never to push or pull the fabric when overlocking. Doing this invariably results in bent or broken needles. Let the feed do the work, and restrict your hands merely to guiding the seamline in the right direction.

4 By guiding the raw edge of the fabric in

to a point just slightly inside the right-hand side of the presser foot, you can avoid cutting off more than absolutely necessary. This is useful if you have only a minimal s.a.

5   Following the edge of a curve is difficult at first and requires practice.

6   When turning sharp corners, run up to the corner and off the end of the fabric; continue running the machine until the chain of thread is long enough for you to be able to lift the presser foot, turn the fabric, and continue down the next straight edge. Afterwards, if necessary, cut the middle of the loop and sew in the thread ends.

7   Remember to clean your overlocker frequently, especially when using knitted fabrics. Felt can gather under the needle-plate surprisingly quickly.

8   Look at the overlocking stitching from time to time to check that the tensions are correct. Compare the look of the overlocking with the diagram illustrating *correct* tension in your instruction book. Any unevenness or looping indicates need for adjustment.

9   As with a sewing machine, the tension discs are closed tightly together when the presser foot is lowered. Therefore, threading through the tension dials must be done with the presser foot *up*, in order that the threads can be properly positioned *between* the tension discs.

10   Angela Thompson's *Complete Book of the Sewing Machine* has a very helpful section on overlockers and also on cut-and-sew. She gives several tips which I did not find in my instruction book but which have proved invaluable.

4 Planning the garment

This really is a case where there are very few hard and fast rules. The only one that I would insist on is that you should *plan*. Work out as precisely as possible exactly what it is that you are going to make, how you are going to make it, and how you are going to neaten the inside of the garment.

PATTERNS (see Chapter 9)
Preferably buy your dressmaking pattern *before* starting to knit the fabric for it. Take out the pattern, separate the pieces (cut *between* the printed cutting lines so that margins are left) and look carefully at the ones you are intending to use. You must decide then whether you are going to knit one long, continuous strip from which you will cut all the pieces, or whether you are going to knit rectangles, each one being just the right width and length to accommodate one piece of pattern. Straight pieces, such as waistbands or cuffs, can be knitted exactly to measurements and so will need no cutting at all. Those who have charting devices can actually knit all the pieces exactly to the size and shape of the pieces of paper pattern. Use simple increasing and decreasing, not the fully-fashioned method, because you may need to cut the fabric, to adjust, after the first fitting. Whether it is worth the extra time taken doing the shaping is something only you can decide.

YARNS
Consider the time of year and the possible weather conditions (or the central heating?) in which you will be wearing this garment or outfit. Are you the kind of person who shivers in the slightest draught or do you tend to feel overheated most of the time? These factors will determine the warmth and thickness of the yarn you choose. Sheer economics will probably govern whether you choose pure silk with cashmere, manufacturers' acrylic leftovers, or something in between. Good quality yarn does tend to look a lot better than poor quality yarn when the knitting is done; it could be false economy to buy the *very* cheap ones.

Then consider the type of garment you are going to make. At this stage, read your pattern envelope very carefully, especially the designer's description of the garment. Is it meant to be close-fitting, semi-fitting or loose-fitting? Does it involve a fair amount of interfacing and lining or is it meant to be soft and flowing? If the garment is intended to be structured, even tailored, then the fabric you are going to knit will need to be fairly firm and stable in texture, with a certain amount of body. You can actually turn a soft, stretchy, rather floppy knit into the appropriate firmer fabric simply by adding a fusible interfacing, either to the whole piece before cutting, or to the separate pieces immediately after cutting. This will reduce the stretch factor and add the necessary body and firmness of texture (see Chapter 6).

If you are aiming at, for instance, a soft, flowing dress, with fullness and draping, perhaps with a loose cardigan type of jacket, then your fabric will obviously need

to be fairly thin, lightweight, soft and flexible. It will probably not be lined at all, or it could, if necessary, have a loose lining, suspended from the neck and armholes. Interfacing would be restricted to small facing pieces.

The paragraph on the pattern envelope back labelled 'Suitable Fabrics' will help you to work out what kind of fabric the designer had in mind. To put it in a rather extreme way, you would not normally consider making an evening blouse from a

length of Harris tweed, nor a winter over-coat from silk-chiffon. *Suitability* is the operative word.

TEXTURES

If you are a fairly experienced knitter, you will probably already have a fairly good idea of what kinds of yarns, combined with which stitch patterns and tensions, are required to produce certain types of fabric. Your choice will, of course, be governed by the type of knitting machine you are using. For example, if your machine is designed for chunky knits, you will probably not be able to turn out the thinner, finer kinds of fabric. Find out, by experimentation, how thick and how fine a yarn your machine will knit satisfactorily.

Fig. 23b   *Close-up of the fabric (Aisin U.K. Ltd)*

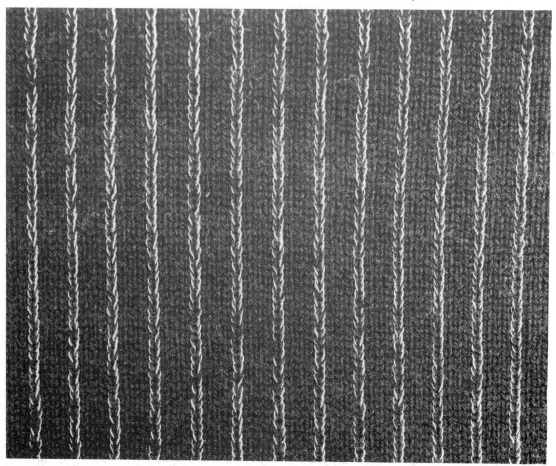

Fig. 24a *Coat. Fabric knitted on a Toyota 901 using Hayfield 3-ply acrylic-nylon. Simulknit reversible; two colours carried on ribber coupling. Fabric well-pressed. All edging bias knitted on single-bed. The coat is completely reversible (Aisin U.K. Ltd)*

Stitch patterns

Those which produce a double-sided fabric are excellent for cut-and-sew work. The resulting firm, flat material makes beautiful unlined coats and jackets and even trousers. As the wrong side looks just as good as the right side, lining becomes unnecessary (see fig. 24(a) and (b)).

Jacquard designs

These are usually very successful and, in fact, you will find many of these on the shelves of dress fabric shops. These make a thicker fabric because they are produced by the main bed *and* the ribber, using a colour changer.

Knit-weaving

Providing you can do it on your machine, this produces a very good firm fabric, with

Fig. 24b *Close-up of the fabric (Aisin U.K. Ltd)*

no sideways stretch at all. This is often considered a suitable fabric for beginning cut-and-sew, but I find that its tendency to stretch lengthwise actually creates .some problems. Fusing an interfacing to the wrong side solves this, and then you have a totally non-stretch fabric to work with. Alternatively, use it sideways.

Plain stocking stitch

Although this tends to roll a lot at the edges, it is usually quite suitable after thorough pressing.

Slip patterns

These are good, and so are Fair Isles, but be careful not to have overlong loops of yarn.

43

Tuck stitches

Provided you accept the fact that the texture of the fabric is going to be altered quite considerably, these stitches are excellent. When pressed, the fabric will be flattened, stretched out into a wider width and consequently its stretch factor will be reduced. This applies particularly when an acrylic fibre is used. Bright courtelle, used for tuck stitch (and many others, of course), takes very well to having a damp cloth and a hot iron applied, and while it alters the 'crunchy' effect of the pattern, it produces an expensive-looking fabric that drapes well. (See figs. 25 and 26(a) and (b); also Chapter 5 on pressing.)

Fig. 25   *Tuck-stitch sample, knitted in bright courtelle, before and after pressing*

Fig. 26b   *Close-up of the fabric (Aisin U.K. Ltd)*

Fig. 26a *Dress. Fabric knitted on a Toyota 901, using Big Ben 3-ply acrylic. Tuck-stitch punch card. Pressed completely flat to give a lightweight open pattern (Aisin U.K. Ltd)*

45

Lace patterns

These can also be perfectly suitable for cut-and-sew work but, again, these will be altered somewhat by the vital pressing (see fig. 27).

Patterns which incorporate very large holes are probably unsuitable, unless you consider actually mounting them on some shop-bought lining fabric, such as chiffon or tulle, or possibly a soft organza, before making up.

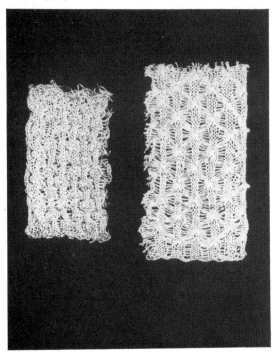

Fig. 27 *Lace sample in bright courtelle, before and after pressing*

Ribbing

If knitted for a welt, this can be avoided in the pressing process. Otherwise, as a main fabric, it will inevitably be stretched in the necessary pressing. Sweater dresses could be made of ribbing left unpressed, but these would either cling rather too tightly to the figure, or end up stretching to fit a much larger size than intended. In any case, these would be better made up by the traditional machine-knitting methods than by cut-and-sew techniques.

Tubular hems

These are ideal for sweater dresses and jackets, long coats, etc., if you like to avoid ribs. These actually give a more expensive, professional-looking finish to the garment but, of course, you still need a ribber with your knitting machine to achieve them.

Very thick fabric

A chunky knitted fabric may well give you problems with your sewing machine and overlocker. There is a limit beyond which needles will break, shuttles jam, uneven stitching will occur, etc. Manufacturers have special heavy-duty machines for these fabrics. Find out, by experimenting on tension squares, how far your own machines can go.

It is worthwhile spending considerable time purely on experimenting. Knit a variety of pieces, approximately 20cm (8in.) square, always making a note of the yarn, the stitch or card, the tension etc., and attaching this information to the piece. Then press half of each square, also making a note of the heat of the iron and whether you used it dry or with steam. You can build up a library of information this way, which will be time-saving when choosing fabrics for your future cut-and-sew work. Try, for instance, knitting a ribby lace fabric in acrylic or bright courtelle and then pressing it thoroughly with a hot iron with steam. You will undoubtedly have 'killed' the fibre, but you may well find the result, although quite different, is very pleasing. Being flatter, thinner and less stretchy, it could be suitable, perhaps, for a blouse with long, full sleeves (see fig. 28).

During the knitting process, try to avoid producing a piece of fabric where the tension at the side edges appears to be looser than in the middle. In other words, where the edges are fluted. Frantic pressing often fails to solve this problem and you simply have to cut your main pieces from

Fig. 28 *Another lace sample, before and after pressing*

the middle of the length, leaving the side strips for waistband, cuffs etc.

Marker threads, placed at both side edges at regular intervals (at about every 20–30 rows), will help you to press the grain of the fabric straight and will ensure accuracy when cutting two identical pattern pieces, such as two sleeves. Do this, whether knitting a length of fabric or rectangular pieces.

CONCLUSION

Looser knitting tension makes for more stretchy, less stable fabric, and consequently you will have more problems in cut-and-sew work. Conversely, tighter tension, which produces firmer, more stable fabric, presents less sewing problems.

However, any knitting can be made more stable, or even totally stable, by fusing an interfacing to it (see Chapter 6). Also, the degree of stretch can be reduced by pressing the fabric well.

In all cases, consider whether the degree of stretch or stability is appropriate to the garment you are thinking of making.

Plan ahead, how you are going to make up the garment and how you are going to give it a neat finish inside.

OTHER HELPFUL HINTS

Make sure you are knitting enough fabric for the garment.

Try to have some spare yarn available after knitting, for making trimmings such as braid, plaiting fringe etc., or even for repairs.

When planning a garment, make sure that all the fabrics involved (the knitted main fabric, any woven fabric used for bands, cuffs etc., the lining fabrics and the interfacing fabrics) are all compatible as regards weight, draping qualities, and laundering or dry-cleaning. For instance, obvious problems would arise if a lining fabric which could only be dry-cleaned, was attached to a knit dress which you would expect to wash by hand.

Remember that not all your pattern pieces have to be cut from your knitted fabric. You could make collars, cuffs and front bands from a matching woven fabric (see fig. 29). On an unlined dress, the neck facing could be made from woven lining material (see fig. 30).

If you intend to quilt your knitted fabric, a pattern of, perhaps, squares or diamonds, incorporated into the knitting, will act as a useful guide when actually doing the quilting.

Fig. 29 *Cuff cut from checked woven poly/cotton gingham sewn to a sleeve made from well-pressed acrylic tuck-stitch knit*

Fig. 30 *Neck facing cut from polyester lining fabric, interlined with Vilene Supershape lightweight*

Always check the fabric's reaction to being pressed.

If you are knitting your fabric in an obvious pattern (of lines, roses, little men or whatever), do be careful to see that you will be able to match this design on the side seams when cutting the pattern pieces. Also, check on what effect you are going to have down centre front and back. For example, a large circle placed at exactly the same distance from the C.F. line and at the same level could be absolutely disastrous!

Consider tubular or U-shaped knitting if you need the fabric to be wide.

Until you are fairly experienced at cut-and-sew work, avoid using very smooth silky yarns for the knitting, as these can unravel more easily when cut.

5 Preparation of the fabric

First of all, run a line of short stitch-length machining, or overlocking, along the unfinished ends of each piece of fabric to prevent unravelling of the knitting during washing and pressing.

WASHING

If you have used Shetland wool, the fabric will need to be washed to remove the oil, which has been added to it to make the knitting process easier, and which has a rather pungent smell. Put the whole lot in the washing machine, on a cool wash with the usual detergent powder and some fabric softener for the final rinse. Alternatively, you can do it by hand, using washing-up liquid and rinsing in fabric softener.

Even if the yarn is not Shetland wool, I still like to soak it thoroughly in warm water (about 40°C) to make quite sure that there will be no further shrinkage when the garment is laundered. This also gives you a chance to see if any of the colours are going to run! If you have a spin drier, use it to remove as much water as possible before hanging up to dry. Drying flat is better, but you may not have space for long lengths. Whether or not you let it dry completely is a matter of judgment. It is possible that it may be more easily and effectively pressed while still slightly damp.

PRESSING

Unless you have knitted a double-sided fabric which is now looking perfectly flat and ready to use, the chances are that your knitting is curling up at the edges, so it now has to be pressed.

One fact that has been made very clear to me, in the cut-and-sew classes I have taught so far, is that nearly everyone is afraid to press their knitted fabrics sufficiently! I have had looks of horror, disbelief and amazement when I have stressed the necessity for more and firmer pressing. This is understandable, because all knitters are constantly warned about the folly of pressing their beautiful knitted textures flat and so ruining them. However, there is a vast difference between sewing up woolly jumpers and what we are aiming at, which is dressmaking with knitted fabrics. If the thought of flattening the texture of your knitting still worries you, then I suggest you go and look at the knitted fabrics in the dress-fabric shops. You will find that they are mostly flat in texture, as, of course, they must be when they are rolled around strips of board and piled up, one on top of the other.

A frequent question is, 'What do you do about acrylics? You surely cannot press those, can you?' The answer is that you *can* and you *must*, because the pressing of seams, collar edges, hems, pocket tops etc. is an essential part of the dressmaking routine. Omit it and you end up with something that looks very obviously home-made. But this pressing *is* going to alter the look of your fabric, so it must *all* be pressed to give an even texture throughout the entire garment. I realise that a completed acrylic jumper can be turned into an immediate disaster when pressed, because it will inevitably be stretched out of shape for ever. Pressing a length of acrylic knitted fabric, however, turns it into a much more suitable medium for dressmaking *because* the irretrievable stretching of the fabric is actually a very good way of stabilising it.

Test pressing

This should have been done on your initial trial square of knitting. Find out whether it reacts best to pressing with a damp cloth, with a steam iron, or with a dry iron. How much heat can you safely use, without, for instance, actually melting any nylon fibre or scorching the wool?

Start with light pressure on the iron, increasing the pressure as necessary.

Press the wrong side of the fabric first. If it seems better to press both sides, press the right side first and then finish on the wrong side.

Never hold the iron still on the fabric for more than a second or you may make an irremovable mark on it. Keep the iron moving slowly with a gentle gliding movement, but not pushing so hard that the fabric changes shape, unless, of course, that is what you intend.

A Teflon iron pad

This is a very helpful aid when pressing knitted fabrics. They are to be found only in the larger department stores, where they are sold by demonstrators. The pad is simply a cover which fits over the sole-plate of the iron and is held in place by a flexible spring band. It appears to be made of white plastic and I find that some of my new students tend to remove it before switching on my iron because, understandably, they think it will melt! It is actually made of a heatproof material which I understand was developed by scientists involved in space exploration. *It has to be used with the iron switched up to its maximum temperature.* It does away with any need for a pressing cloth because it will not produce a shine on the fabric, neither will it allow scorching. I find it ideal for ironing on fusible interfacings and bonding agents, because any stickiness

is easily wiped off the cover with a damp cloth. Use the cover preferably with a steam iron, giving plenty of steam. If your iron is dry, spray the fabric with water first. It does have quite amazing properties, including the ability to press velvet on the right side without ruining it! With this aid, it *is* possible to carry out effective pressing on acrylics without necessarily 'killing' the fabric.

Directional pressing

This is necessary if the knitting emerges from washing or soaking with a slight bias twist in it. If your knitted piece looks like fig. 31(a), you should press with a diagonal movement from A to D until the rows of knitting lie at right angles to the selvedges, as in fig. 31(b). You may need to use more pressure on the iron than usual, and a fair amount of pushing and pulling will be necessary.

Fig. 31 *Pressing and pushing in the direction of the arrow (a) to achieve a straight grain (b)*

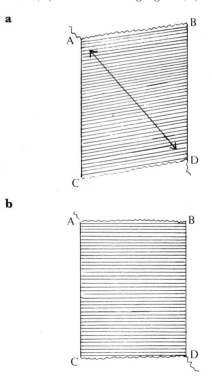

If the knitted piece has fluted edges, then you should push in a lengthwise direction with the iron, up and down the central area, in order to stretch it to match the edges. Then press from near the centre, outwards towards the edges, as in fig. 32. This is not always successful and, during the cooling off period, which you should always allow for before starting to cut, the fabric may return to its previous state. In this case, use the middle of the strip for cutting a main garment piece and keep the edge strips for waistbands, cuffs etc.

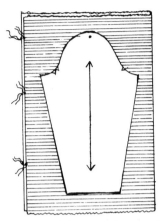

Fig. 33a *Folded fabric for cutting two sleeves*

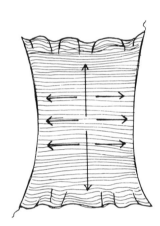

Fig. 32 *Pressing to counteract 'fluted' edges*

Width and length

If a piece of knitting has been calculated to be wide enough to cut two identical pattern pieces (such as two sleeves) from it, side by side, then fold the piece in half lengthwise, matching the thread markers on the selvedges. Press the piece as it lies, doubled. Be very careful not to stretch the folded edge (see fig. 33(a)). Do the same if you are going to use, for example, a half back of a dress (see fig. 33(b)).

If pressing one very long strip of knitting, allow to cool and then roll it on to a piece of stiff board (even better, one of the cardboard cylinders in which posters are mailed) which is slightly longer than the width of the fabric. Ideally, leave it on this to settle for a day or two before cutting out.

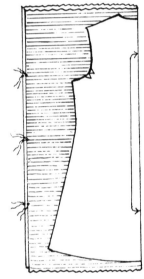

Fig. 33b *Folded fabric for cutting the whole back of a dress*

Pressing during garment construction

See Chapter 6 for instructions on fusing interfacing.

Press all seams as soon as they have been machined. Use the seam roller if there seems any possibility that the seam allowances will make an impression on the right side. To do this, simply put the roller on the ironing board and then centre the seam to be pressed along the top of the roller; when the iron is laid on top, only the seam itself will be pressed and not the seam allowances.

Use the sleeve board for pressing sleeves and sleeve hems. Slip the pressing mitt over the end for pressing shoulders, but this is a delicate area and is better avoided unless absolutely necessary.

Use the tailor's ham for pressing curved seams, necks, collars etc.

Use the pounding block for hems, pocket edges, collar edges etc. Press one section at a time, with plenty of steam or with a damp pressing cloth; then immediately bring the flat side of the block down hard on the edge which is still hot and damp. Hold it there for five seconds. The untreated wood will absorb the steam, and the edge will be set in a firm crease.

6 Stabilising

During the construction of cut-and-sew clothes, there is usually some point (or several points) at which one needs to reduce, or even to eliminate totally, the stretch quality of the knitted fabric, in order to make sure that the garment maintains its intended shape. Here are two examples of this:

Collars are usually stabilised by the use of an interfacing, so that they will keep their shape and the neck seamline will not stretch.

The vertical front edges of an unlined jacket can be stabilised by the addition of interfaced facings, or by the attachment of braid or ribbon to the edges. If these front edges were not stabilised, they would very soon stretch and sag.

Be prepared to stabilise in the following areas, depending, of course, on the design of the garment you are making:

Collars
Cuffs
Facings
Pockets
Waistbands
Yokes
Some hems
Front, or back, openings (with or without attached bands) where buttons, snaps, ties etc., may be used for fastening. Also interface where no fastenings are to be added.
Any seam which runs roughly in the same direction as the rows of knitting, i.e. across the knitting. For example,

shoulder, back neck and yoke seams, where stretching would spoil the shape of the garment.

I have found the following stabilising agents to be the most helpful in cut-and-sew work. The addition of these can convert a sloppy, difficult to handle knit into a firmer, still pliable fabric, which is less likely to unravel.

Fusible knitted nylon
(See Appendix I for U.S.A. brand name)
This is a very thin layer of finely knitted nylon with an adhesive backing. The width is usually around 142cm (56in.). Stockists of this interfacing in the U.K. are rather few and far between at present. Ask around and be prepared to buy by mail order. If you have a thriving knitting-machine club which includes a number of cut-and-sew enthusiasts, you could try asking your local draper to stock it for you. The name of one manufacturer is listed at the end of the book and he will supply the address of your nearest stockist on application.

To apply fusible knitted nylon
Place it with the adhesive-covered side down, on to the wrong side of your knitted fabric. If you are using a Teflon iron-cover, make sure that the heat is turned up to the highest point. If not, use a very thin, dry cloth or tissue paper between the iron and the nylon interfacing; this avoids any danger of melting the nylon or of getting the adhesive on the sole-plate of the iron. The use of steam from the iron does help,

although moisture is not essential with this interfacing.

Use a gentle, gliding motion but take great care not to alter the shape of the pieces.

This interfacing will add body and give stability to your knitted fabric, reducing but not eliminating its stretch quality (see fig. 34). I have found it particularly valuable for reducing the possibility of any sagging or seating in skirts. Depending on the effect you want to achieve, you may choose to interface *all* the knitted fabric in the garment, but bear in mind that if you fuse an entire length of knit to an equal length of interfacing, there is some danger of getting the grain slightly off-straight which will spoil the look of the finished garment. It is safer to fuse short lengths, or, having cut the pattern pieces in the knit, to cut the same pieces again in interfacing and then to fuse the twin pieces together before starting to assemble the garment.

Fig. 34 *Knitted fabric before and after interfacing with fusible knitted nylon*

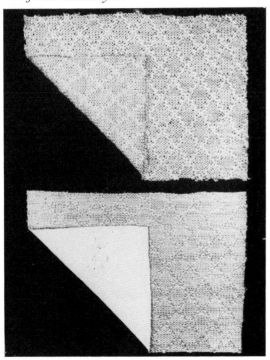

Be very precise and accurate when doing this, in order to avoid confusion during the sewing process.

You can, providing the seams are sufficiently neatened, use this type of interfacing as a lining, but its appearance is not acceptable to everyone, and it is usually preferable to add a sewn-in lining in the case of a coat or jacket.

Vilene New Supershape Iron-on interfacings

These are non-woven, non-knitted, fusible interfacings, made principally of various synthetic fibres bonded together in sheet form and then backed with an adhesive. Width is 90cm (36in.). These are the four types I recommend:

New Supershape Iron-on. Lightweight. White. No. 300.

New Supershape Iron-on. Lightweight. Charcoal. No. 301.

New Supershape Iron-on. Medium weight. White. No. 302.

New Supershape Iron-on. Heavy weight. White. No. 303.

These interfacings are quite different from the old, rather stiff and unyielding Vilenes. They have a definite grainline which must be followed when placing your pattern pieces, because they have a degree of stretch, both across the width and on the bias. There is almost no stretch, however, when the interfacing is pulled lengthwise. So, this stretch/non-stretch quality can be used to stabilise your knitting, either partly or totally.

Some examples of this are:

1 An applied band, down the front edge of a jacket, would be interfaced with the grain running up and down the length of the band, so that it could not sag lengthwise.

2 A similar lengthwise strip could be cut to fit a yoke *across* the shoulders, preventing it stretching and so falling off the shoulders and down the arms.

3 The whole of the front of a jacket could

Fig. 35 *Jacket. Fabric knitted on a Jones Lacemaker with Twilley's ' Flaxen' yarn, using a tuck-stitch on tension 8, producing a zigzag pattern. Vilene Supershape medium weight used in the jacket fronts, collar and pockets. Fold-a-Band used in the sleeve and jacket hems. Completely cut-and-sewn to a Style dressmaking pattern (The Vilene Organisation)*

56

be interfaced, with the stretch going across (the grain lengthwise), so that a certain amount of give widthways would be retained, although the fabric would have been considerably stabilised.

4 If, for some reason, a piece of knitted fabric needs to be *completely* stable, two layers of the lightweight Supershape could be applied, using the grain in both directions.

These examples indicate clearly that, by using these interfacings in a carefully calculated way, your knitted fabrics can be used to make a wide variety of clothes, including coats and jackets (see figs. 35 and 36).

Vilene Supershape Iron-on is stocked by most drapers, but do make sure that you are buying the Supershape range of Vilene interfacings. Vilene also make two other fusibles, called Firm Iron-on and Soft Iron-on. These have no grain and produce a much crisper finish which is not so suitable for knitted fabrics although they can sometimes be useful for stand-up collars or wide belts, etc. Not all retailers seem to be aware of these differences, so be warned!

When buying Vilene Supershape, choose the weight appropriate to the thickness of your knitted fabric, bearing in mind that the lightweight one does not adhere so well to large areas of knit. Generally, I find the medium weight most useful but would use the heavy weight for chunky knits. Also, remember not to use it at all for interlining a skirt (as suggested in the case of the fusible knitted nylon interfacing), because the bonding of the fibres would probably start to disintegrate with the constant friction and stretching involved.

Use the lightweight Supershape for interfacing any facings cut from woven fabrics such as polyester lining, cotton poplin or silk.

Make sure that you buy whatever length is required to place your pattern pieces correctly with the grainline of this Vilene. For example, long front facings should not be placed across the width.

Fig. 36 *Dress. Fabric knitted on a Jones Lacemaker with Twilley's ' Wisper' yarn. Vilene Supershape used in neck and armhole facings and Fold-a-Band behind the pleats. Completely cut-and-sewn to a Style dressmaking pattern (The Vilene Organisation)*

To apply Vilene Supershape interfacings

1 Always test on each fabric before use, using spare pieces, to make sure that the feel is what you require, and to note the effect of using the grain in different directions.

2 Cut the interfacing, using your paper pattern pieces, not the knitted pieces you have already cut out, because they may have stretched a little out of shape.

3 Place the rough-feeling, slightly shiny side (the adhesive side) down on to the wrong side of the fabric.

4 Cover with a *damp* pressing cloth.

5 Press with a hot, dry iron, *until the cloth is dry.* Use a pressing-up-and-down action at first, and follow with a gentle, gliding action. Take care not to push the knitted fabric out of shape.

6 Leave to cool before handling.

These interfacings, once correctly applied and sewn into the garment, are washable and dry-cleanable.

Fusible woven cotton muslin

This is simply a thin, rather loosely-woven cotton muslin with an adhesive backing. Staflex is one of the trade names for it (see p. 113 for U.S.A. equivalent). It is obtainable from some drapers, but you may have to hunt for it. Since the advent of the new Vilene Supershapes I have used it less often, but it is still useful when you wish to eliminate the stretch factor altogether from the knitted fabric, e.g. in a collar band. Use it mainly for small areas where it will eventually be secured by machine-stitching, because, when applied to knits, it may not continue to adhere well throughout laundering.

To apply, place the muslin, glue-side (shiny side) down on to the wrong side of the knit. Either cover with pattern paper or use the Teflon iron-pad, because otherwise a certain amount of glue will stick to the sole-plate of the iron. Press well. Moisture is not necessary for this one.

Cotton tape

Buy this in approximately 0.6cm ($\frac{1}{4}$in.) width and, before using, shrink it well by soaking in boiling water and then pressing with a hot iron. Use it for stabilising seams which go *across* the knitting, such as shoulder, back neck and shoulder yoke seams (see fig. 37). To do this, first cut your lengths of tape, using your paper pattern as a guide (*not* the pieces of knit which you have already cut and which may well have stretched). Cut the pieces of tape to fit the entire length of the seamline being stabil-

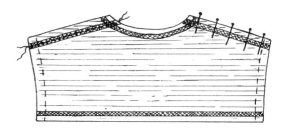

Fig. 37 *Tape stabilising the crosswise seams on a yoke*

ised, including the s.a.'s. Pin these into position as shown in fig. 37, centring the tapes exactly on the seamlines. If the knit has stretched, make it contract so that it does fit the tapes! Use plenty of pins, placed across the seamline. Machine along the centre of each length of tape, using threads which match the knit, removing each pin as the machine foot reaches it. When attaching the front and back of the garment, keep the taped side uppermost and follow the same machine line exactly.

Vilene Wundatrim

Use this narrow bonding medium (sold in three widths) for holding stabilising-tape, ribbon-trimming etc., in position before machining, instead of pinning. Carefully place the Wundatrim in position, cover by placing the tape or ribbon directly on top and press lightly with a dry iron first. Then finish by pressing again with a damp cloth.

Fig. 38 *Blouson jacket. Fabric knitted on a Jones Lacemaker with Twilley's 'Bubbly 100' mercerised cotton yarn. Vilene Supershape used in collar and cuffs and Fold-a-Band in the pleats and front edges. Completely cut-and-sewn to a Style dressmaking pattern (The Vilene Organisation)*

Vilene Fold-a-Band

Use this fusible interfacing band for giving perfectly straight, sharp edges to front-bands, cuffs, pocket tops, pleats, waistbands and some hems (see fig. 38). The width is limited to 3cm ($1\frac{1}{4}$in.) but I find this quite adequate for most purposes. Place it on the W.S., lining the central slits up with the fold-line. Press with a hot iron and a damp cloth, then leave to cool. Vilene recommend the lightweight version for most jobs except waistbands, which require the heavier weight. If using a chunky-knit fabric, you may find the waistband weight better for front-bands, cuffs etc., where the lightweight will possibly not adhere well. Top-stitching, through the band, is advisable to ensure that the Fold-a-Band remains in place.

Non-stretch braids and ribbons

These have a decorative purpose, but also count as stabilisers when used to stop the edges of knit-fabric clothes from sagging and stretching (see fig. 85).

Woven fabrics

Woven fabrics which match, tone or contrast with the knitted fabric can also be used as stabilisers. For example, where a knitted coat is given neck- and front-bands cut from woven wool flannel, the woven neck-band (because it does not stretch) automatically stabilises the neck seamline; the front-bands, being woven and not knitted, will not sag downwards, but will stabilise the front edges of the coat (see fig. 39). A shoulder yoke will keep its shape beautifully if cut from purchased, woven needlecord, toning with the rest of the dress which has been knitted in fine wool.

Fig. 39 *Close-up of photograph on front cover. Front edges of coat and pocket-top stabilised by applied bands of contrasting woven fabric*

Woven fabrics can also be used to stabilise when they are added to a knit as a backing. This backing can be decorative as well: think of a very holey lace-knit in black mounted on to peach-tinted silk. In the case of a firm, non-transparent knit, you could use woven, fusible cotton muslin, to give extra stability around the edges, or in other small areas of the garment such as pockets.

Note Learning how, when and where to use stabilising methods is, I am sure, the most important factor in successful cut-and-sew work.

7 Experiments and alterations

EXPERIMENTS

You may very well find that there are several mental barriers to be overcome before you feel sufficiently confident to tackle a cut-and-sew project. For some knitters, the prospect of actually cutting their knitted fabric, and the possible dire consequences of doing so, are sufficiently off-putting for them to avoid it like the plague!

To overcome this fear, I suggest that you put aside a couple of hours for pure experimentation. Collect up some of your machine-knitted tension swatches, particularly ones knitted to a fairly firm texture. For the moment, avoid very lacy patterns and ribs; you can try them later.

Cutting

Start by cutting one of your pieces in half in a lengthwise direction, and then cut one of the halves across widthways. Now, just handle these pieces *gently*. You will find that, short of actually pulling them about quite drastically, the knitting will not disintegrate. Naturally, fairly strong pulling widthways will probably produce ladders or slipped stitches, but you are not going to do that. The point to remember is that, whenever you have just cut a piece of knitting, you must always handle it gently until some form of stabilising process in the making up of the garment has made it secure.

Pressing

Now try pressing your tension swatches (see Chapter 5 on pressing). Note how this changes the texture and possibly the size of the pieces. Experiment with less heat, more heat, using a dry cloth, using a damp cloth, and try the Teflon iron-pad if you have one. Think of what you might be going to make with your fabric. Because you are going to be dressmaking with it, it needs to be fairly flat and stable.

Seaming

Next, cut two lengthwise pieces of knitting (to the same length) and pin them exactly together (see p. 87 and fig. 67). Now machine a seam 1.5cm ($\frac{5}{8}$in.) from the long edges. As you are experimenting, sew your first seam with a st. stit. and, when finished, give it a good, sharp stretch from one end of the seam to the other. You may well find that the thread used for the machining has snapped, thus proving that a st. stit. seam is not a good idea for stretchy fabrics. Do it again, this time using a small ZZ (1 to $1\frac{1}{2}$ stitch width) and a medium stitch length. Stretch this seam and, in most cases, it will *not* snap. If it does, it may be because you have an all-cotton thread in the machine or that the tension is too tight. (See Chapter 3 on threads for machining; also for tension adjustment.)

Try, now, machining a seam across the width of the knitting, in the same way as you did the lengthwise pieces, pinning carefully first. This time, you are almost certain to find that the seamline has stretched quite considerably more than its original width. This shows you that, whenever you are faced with a seam going across the knitting, one of the two pieces being sewn together must be stabilised (see Chapter 6 on stabilising) in order to avoid ending up with a mis-shapen garment.

Having now built up your confidence, you could make further progress by trying out, on more spare pieces of knitting, some of the sewing processes in Chapter 12. For example, discover how to attach a facing, cut from interfaced woven fabric, to a piece of knitted fabric. However, you may prefer to enlarge your experience by cutting and altering some knitted clothes you, or your family, have grown out of or cast aside for various reasons.

ALTERATIONS

This section deals with some suggested alterations, many of which would be useful if you have a young and growing family. Outgrown children's clothes can be made wider and longer by cutting them and inserting strips of contrasting knitted fabric. Likewise, items discarded by adults can often be cut down to fit the younger ones. This can all be valuable experience in cut-and-sew work, and will give you confidence to embark on more ambitious projects.

Making a sweater smaller in width
(see fig. 40)

First, try the sweater on the person it is intended for, with the sweater inside out. Pin out the excess fullness, equally on the two sides, from the waist up to the under-arm and continuing, if necessary, along the arm seam. Take care not to make it too tight. Also take care that the pins do no harm when the sweater is being taken off!

Now mark the pinned line with dots up each side of the sweater, on the wrong side, preferably with your Pikaby marking pen or with a moistened coloured pencil. If this does not show on the fabric, mark the line with a needle and contrasting thread. Then re-pin, at right angles to the seamline, pinning the fabric together *on* the seamline, as in fig. 67.

Stitch the seamline on your sewing machine, using a 1 to $1\frac{1}{2}$ width ZZ or, if your machine can do it, one of the seaming-and-overlocking stitches. (Take care to remove the pins before the needle hits them.) In the latter case, it may be preferable to cut off the excess seam allowance before stitching; otherwise cut it off after

Fig. 40 *Reducing the width of a sweater*

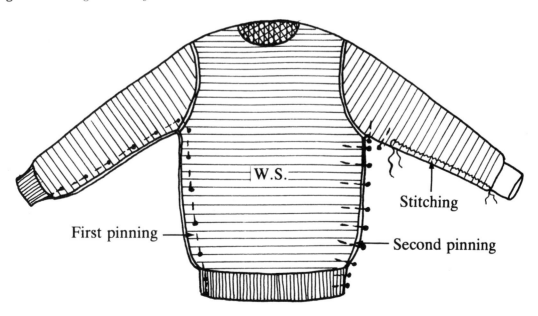

First pinning

W.S.

Stitching

Second pinning

stitching. If you have a domestic overlocking machine, use it either to overlock the edges after machine stitching the seam, or, to seam, cut off and overlock all in one operation if your overlocker will do that. You will probably have to neaten, by hand, the ends of the seams, which might otherwise show on the right side.

Adding width to a sweater (see figs. 41 and 42)

1 Measure the person for whom the altered sweater is intended, around the chest. To this measurement, add anything between 5 and 15cm (2 and 6in.) room for movement, depending on how loose the sweater is required to be.

Subtract the present circumference of the sweater from this sum. The answer, divided by two, is the width of the strip which you will need to put into each side seam and sleeve seam. (If this is going to make the sleeves too baggy, taper the sleeve strips from underarm to wrist.) Add 4cm (1½in.) to the width for s.a.'s

Example: Person measures 86cm (34in.) (chest circumference)

Add 10cm (4in.) room for movement: 86cm (34in.) + 10cm (4in.) = 96cm (38in.)

Sweater measures 84cm (33in.) (circumference at chest level)

Extra fabric to be added is 96cm (38in.) − 84cm (33in.) = 12cm (5in.)

12cm (5in.) divided by 2 = 6cm (2½in.)

6cm (2½in.) + 4cm (1½in.) (seam allowances) = <u>10cm</u> (4in.)

So, in this example, 10cm (4in.) will be the width of the strips, of which you will need two for the body and two for the arms.

2 Measure the present side and underarm seams to determine the lengths of the strips. If you are cutting these strips from a length of knitted fabric, you will need to include an underarm s.a. and a hem allowance in the lengths. You can, of course, knit these strips to the exact finished measurements and thus dispense with s.a.'s altogether, except for 2cm (¾in.) on the width to allow for your new strips overlapping the sweater fabric by 1cm (⅜in.) on each side.

3 Cut out the side and sleeve seams from the sweater by cutting neatly on either side of them. (If the original seams are easy to unravel, then do that instead.)

Fig. 41 *Adding width to a sweater: side and underarm seams removed*

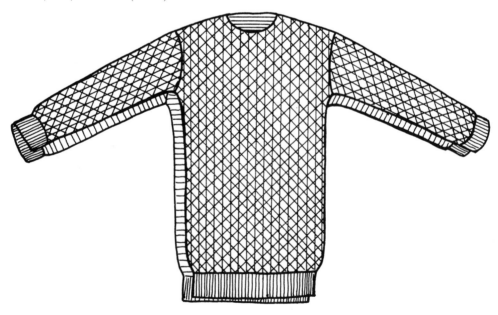

64

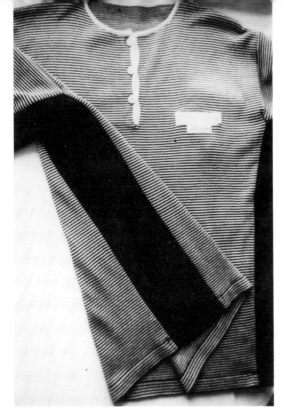

Fig. 42 *Contrast piece inserted (the T-shirt and inserted strips in this illustration are industrially knitted, but exactly the same alteration can be done using domestic machine-knitted fabrics)*

4 Undo the armhole seam at the under-arm point for about 6cm (2½in.).

5 Pin the strips in position and stitch by machine (see Chapter 12 for seaming methods).

6 Complete the armhole seam, following the usual underarm curve.

7 Trim away any surplus fabric at the underarm point and neaten with overlocking.

Shortening a sweater (see fig. 43)

1 Try the sweater on the person for whom it is intended. Decide, by pinning out a tuck evenly all round, how much fabric you will need to remove, both from the body and from the sleeves.

2 Cut the sweater, all round, 1.5cm (⅝in) above the top of the ribbing on the body and on the sleeves.

3 Remove the required even depth from the cut edge of the body and from the

sleeve ends, but remember to leave on an extra 1.5cm (⅝in.) for the s.a. which will be required for joining the ribbing back on again.

Note A problem arises here, in that the seams you are going to stitch will be running across the knitting, i.e. this seam is going to stretch. If you are using a domestic overlocker, the problem will be minimal, but if you are using an ordinary sewing machine you will have to take some steps to avoid having a stretched-out seamline. In this particular case, you cannot stabilise either the ribbing or the main fabric by taping one of them, because the bottom of the sweater must be able to stretch in order to get it on. I suggest that the answer here is to use an *ease-stitching* line.

4 Ease-stitch by setting the machine to do the longest possible st. stit. (perhaps with the top tension tightened up a little) and running a line of this long straight stitching along the seamline of both pieces of fabric to be joined, i.e. a line round the bottom of the cut sweater and another along the top of the ribbing band. You will find that you can fairly easily pull up on *either* the needle thread of this stitching or the bobbin

Fig. 43 *Shortening a sweater by removing strips above the ribbing*

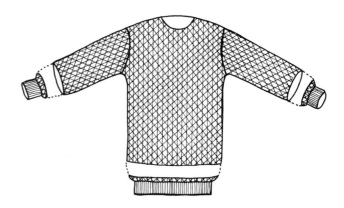

thread; it could, in fact, be gathered, but you do not want to gather it, only to pull it up sufficiently to make it lie flat and unstretched. Do this to both the bottom of the sweater and to the ribbing until they are roughly the same in circumference.

5 Pin the two pieces together, with the pins at right angles to the edge. Then stitch with combined seaming and overlocking (if your machine does that), or with a narrow ZZ followed by oversewing the raw edges. The long st. stit.'s should hold the fabric sufficiently to prevent it from stretching. Once the seam is completed, it can be stretched and the straight stitching will undoubtedly snap; this does not matter at all because its job has been accomplished and it is no longer needed.

Repeat this procedure for the sleeves.

Note If this method is unsuccessful, or if you already have a crosswise seam which has stretched, it can be retrieved by threading Shirlastic through it and pulling up the Shirlastic until the seam lies flat.

Lengthening a sweater (see fig. 44(a))
This can be done by inserting plain bands of knitted fabric (to tone or contrast with the main fabric of the sweater) into the body and sleeves. It usually looks best if the stripe around the body lines up with those on the sleeves, but you can vary them in any way you please.

1 Work out the depth of the bands by

Fig. 44 *Lengthening a sweater by inserting contrasting bands of knitted fabric*

a

b

c

d

66

deciding how much extra length you actually need in the body and in the sleeves. Add 6cm (2½in.) for s.a.'s, which will be the standard 1.5cm (⅝in.), unless you are going to knit your bands exactly to the right width, in which case you will need only 2cm (¾in.) extra depth to allow the bands to overlap the sweater fabric by 1cm (⅜in.).

2 Cut the sweater, as shown, having planned where the inserted bands are to be.
3 Pin and machine the bands into the sweater, taking the same precautions to avoid stretching as when shortening.

Once you have mastered this lengthening technique, you can go on to experiment with variations on the straight bands of additional fabric (see fig. 44(b), (c) and (d)).

If you have no overlocking machine and you find the problem of stretched seams insurmountable when using a sewing machine, then knit the bands exactly to the correct shape and depth and apply them to the cut edge of the sweater, on the right side. Stitch by hand with a backstitch in a matching colour.

NORWEGIAN SWEATERS

Passed on to me by a Danish friend who learned it as a child, and explained fully in the Dale Yarn Company's *Knit Your Own Norwegian Sweaters*, this method was designed by hand-knitters, using circular needles, to avoid the difficulties involved in shaping Fair Isle knits.

The body of the garment is knitted as a straight tube from hem to neck level and cast off straight. The sleeves, either tubular or flat, are also cast off straight and then sewn into vertical slits cut at opposite sides of the top of the body tube (see fig. 45). The straight shoulder seams are stitched up and a ribbed band applied to the cut out neck. For a cardigan, the front is cut up the middle and the edges enclosed in a folded ribbed band, or stitched to a single ribbed band with the seams on the R.S. covered

by strips of embroidered cotton ribbon. The latter has the added advantage of stabilising the front edges as well as hiding the seam. Pewter buttons or decorative clasps are sewn on for fastening (see fig. 81).

This method is interesting from the cut-and-sew angle, but the problems involved in producing tubular Fair Isle probably make it inapplicable to most machine-knitters. It is very useful, however, for those who take the trouble to knit Fair Isle by hand, and also for those who use the quiet 'Simple-Frame'; I am assured by Dr. Patrick Reilly that it is perfectly possible to knit tubular Fair Isle on this, although the limited number of stitches, on even the largest model, would restrict the circumference to 91cm (36in.).

Fig. 45 *Norwegian sweater showing cut-and-sew armhole*

$\mathbf{8}$ Body measurements

Choosing your dressmaking pattern in the right size (see Chapter 9) depends largely on the accuracy with which you measure the figure, which I am assuming here is your own.

TAKING MEASUREMENTS
When taking your measurements, follow this routine:

a Take the measurements over underwear only.

b Tie a piece of narrow tape tightly around the waist to define the waistline.

c Stand in front of a long mirror, so that you can check that, for example, the tape-measure is level all round when measuring the bust, that the hip measurement is being

taken at the widest part, etc.

d Be strictly honest!

The first five measurements (see fig. 46(a) and (b)) are those upon which your correct pattern type and size are based. These should be compared with the size charts in the pattern catalogue.

Bust (1) Around fullest part of bust, keeping tape level across the back.

High-bust (2) Directly under the arms, all round, keeping tape level. (*Note* the difference between these two measurements. If the bust measurement is more than about 6cm ($2\frac{1}{2}$in.) bigger than the high-bust measurement, you are probably wearing a C, D or DD-cup bra. In this case, choose your pattern by your high-bust measurement and then carry out an alteration to the paper pattern to make more room for the bust (see Chapter 9).

Fig. 46 *Measurements to be taken*

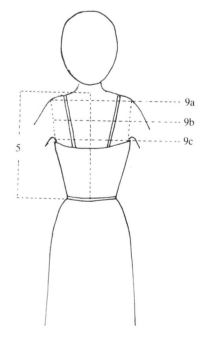

68

Waist (3) Measure where the tape has settled on your waistline.

Hips (4) Around the fullest part. Look at your sideways profile to determine exactly where this is. Place a pin across the side seam to mark this level.

Back waist length (5) From base of neck at back, straight down to the waist tape.

The following measurements should be compared with those of the pattern pieces, to see if alterations need to be made, e.g. to the width across the shoulders, to the sleeve length etc. (fig. 46(a), (b), (c) and (d)).

Stomach (6) Look at the sideways profile and take the measurement around the fullest part. Place a pin on the side seam at this level.

Waist level to stomach level (7) Take this down side seam from waist-tape to the pin marking the stomach level.

Waist level to hip level (8) Also down side seam from waist-tape to pin marking hip level.

Note This can vary between 7 and 26cm (3 and 10½in.) depending on height and type of figure.

Back shoulder widths (9)
a Between tops of arms, across back of neck, with arms held at sides.
b Distance between armhole seamlines, across shoulder-blades, with arms held at sides.
c Distance between underarm points, *with arms stretched forwards.*

Shoulder to bust (10) Distance from neck end of shoulder seam to bust point. First, decide which shoulder is the higher (if either) and measure from that one.

Front waist length (11) From neck end of the same shoulder, over the bust point and down to the waist-tape.

Sleeve length (12) (Elbow must be bent whilst taking this measurement.)
a End of shoulder seam to elbow point.
b Elbow to wrist bone.

c

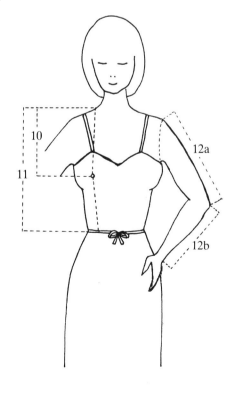

d

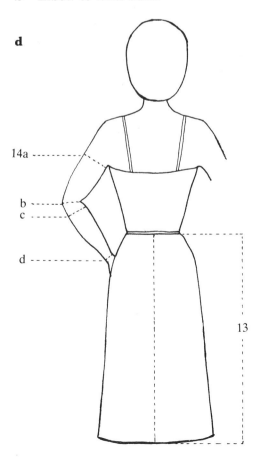

Note I do not recommend taking the underarm sleeve measurement. As one cannot be sure, usually, how far up into the armpit the armhole will actually come, this measurement can be very inaccurate. The top-of-the-arm to wrist measurement, taken over a bent elbow, is more certain.

Skirt length (13) Always take this down C.B. This measurement will vary depending on the type of skirt and current fashion.

Arm circumference (14)
Measure this at the following points:
a the top, at underarm level;
b the elbow, measured with bent elbow;
c 5cm (2in.) below the elbow;
d wrist level.

These are necessary only if chubby arms are a problem or if the sleeves are to be very close-fitting.

Write all these measurements in a note-book and keep it readily accessible for whenever you have to check pattern pieces (see Chapter 9). Add to the list a note of any adjustments you are likely to have to carry out; for example, 'Enlarge at bust level', 'Lengthen sleeves', 'Shorten skirt length', etc. (see Chapter 9 for adjustments). Make a note of the date of recording these measurements and re-check them occasionally.

9 Patterns

If your previous experience happens to include a pattern-cutting course, you may well be able to design and cut your own patterns. Otherwise you will have to rely on being able to buy patterns which have been professionally designed and graded to your own size.

CHOOSING A PATTERN
When choosing, consider the following points:

Style
Is it suitable for the fabric you have knitted or are going to knit? If not, can it be rendered suitable by pressing or by the addition of woven fabrics, fusible interfacings etc.? Is this style actually suitable for you and your figure, shape and lifestyle?

Type of sizing
Most of us are what the pattern manufacturers term Misses, but those whose back-neck-to-waist lengths are shorter than average, and whose hips and waists are large in proportion to bust, come into the Half-size category. Women's patterns are for those with a full-bust measurement of 107cm (42in.) or more, combined with normal or long back waist measurement. Misses Petite or Junior Petite are designed for the smaller, well-proportioned but less fully developed figure. Children's designs are graded in groups which refer to particular stages of their development: Babies, Toddlers, etc. These categories do vary a little depending on the manufacturer. For example, Vogue have discarded Women

but have enlarged the category Misses to include larger sizes, though only up to 122cm (48in.) bust. Butterick continue with Women's up to 137cm (54in.) bust. To be sure of choosing the correct size, consult the tables on the end pages of the counter catalogues.

Actual size of pattern
After taking and recording your measurements (see Chapter 8), make sure that your pattern will fit you as nearly as possible. Choose any design which includes your top half by your bust size; waist and hips are easily altered. Choose a skirt, culottes or trousers pattern by your hip size. Remember, however, that those who take more than a B-cup bra size may require a size smaller than their bust size indicates, but a bust-enlargement alteration to the pattern will then be required.

The pattern manufacturers
There are many basic similarities between patterns produced by the principal distributors in this country: Vogue, Butterick, Simplicity, Style and McCall. The German Burda patterns require extra care because s.a.'s are not included and have to be added at the cutting stage. Patterns offered in magazines, at less than usual cost, occasionally have less than adequate instructions.

The pattern designer's intentions
Always read the description of the garment, either in the shop's counter catalogue or on

the back of the pattern envelope, and note the specific terms used. 'Very loose-fitting' means exactly that; the garment will fit only where it touches and will include a lot of room for ease (movement). At the other end of the scale, 'close-fitting' defines a garment which will fit the figure closely with very limited room for movement. Remember, too, that terms such as 'Very Easy', 'Fast and Easy', 'Make it tonight' etc., are for very simple clothes with few seams and limited fitting: pullover dresses with elasticated waists are not always complimentary to every type of figure.

Your ability and equipment

If you really are a beginner, it would be wiser to start with a simple skirt or top and to build up your experience gradually. If your sewing machine will only do a st. stit., you may be limited by your inability to sew a seam which will stretch. Remember, though, that you can still make clothes in which the stretch has been either eliminated or considerably reduced, by the use of interfacings and/or linings.

Patterns labelled 'For Knits'

These would seem to be very suitable for use by machine knitters. Bear in mind, however, that these are designs which enable non-machine knitters to make up their woollies by dressmaking methods. Machine knitters should be able to make this type of garment more satisfactorily by the usual knitting machine processes. These patterns generally are cut with less room for movement included in the measurements, because they depend on the stretch factor in the fabric for comfort and for a close fit.

Designer patterns

These are labelled with the designer's name: Jean Muir, Pierre Balmain, etc. They are usually rather more expensive and do require a good basic knowledge of dressmaking, but, because the pattern cutting is more detailed and the sewing instructions are more comprehensive, they constitute excellent lessons in the craft. Offset their initial cost by using them several times in different fabrics and with slight variations.

CHECKING PAPER PATTERNS

Never simply lay your pattern on the fabric and start to cut, unless you happen to be one of the few whose measurements line up precisely with a standard pattern size. Having taken the 14 measurements described in Chapter 8, check them against the actual widths and lengths of the pattern pieces. With time and experience, you will be able to reduce this process to checking only those measurements where your own body varies from the normal. For example, I know that I always have to add to body and sleeve length because I am taller than average. In addition, where the design is close-fitting, I know I shall have to add considerably to the waist circumference to allow for the extra girth acquired in passing years.

Assuming that you have bought your pattern in the right size and for your particular figure type, your adjustments should not need to be too drastic. Decide which alterations you will need and note them alongside your measurement list.

The following list covers those I have found to be most often required.

1 Enlargement of waist and hips on patterns bought by bust size (p. 76).
2 Enlargement of waist on patterns (for skirts, trousers etc.) bought by hip size (p. 76).
3 Shortening or lengthening of skirts (p. 74).
4 Enlargement of bust for those who take more than a B-cup bra (pp. 77–8).
5 Lengthening of bodice pieces for those with extra long back neck-to-waist lengths (p. 74).
6 'Dowager's Hump' alteration for those with rounded backs (pp. 79–80).
7 Raising or lowering of bust point on styles where a bust dart is included (p. 75).

Dress — made from finely knitted acrylic in tuck stitch, from a Vogue American Designer (John Anthony) pattern. The shawl collar is interfaced with Vilene Supershape.

Blouson jacket — made from pure wool in a plain chunky knit, from a Style pattern. The front is fastened with a chunky plastic zip. The hems of the jacket and sleeves are elasticated, and the whole garment lined with cream fur fabric. There are pockets in the side seams.

Track suit — knitted with 1 strand acrylic bouclé and 1 strand acrylic 2/30, plated; plain knitting used on the purl side. The pattern used was Vogue, and purchased flat ribbing was used for the waistband and the cuffs of the top. The trousers have an elasticated waist.

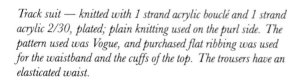

8 Raising or lowering of elbow ease or elbow dart on a close-fitting sleeve (p. 74).
9 Increasing width of a close-fitting sleeve (pp. 76–7).

ADJUSTING PAPER PATTERNS

Bear the following points in mind when altering paper patterns.

1 If the pattern is printed in one size only, simply separate the pieces by cutting through the tissue between them; it is not necessary to cut carefully around each piece on the cutting line. The extra tissue could be useful for marking extensions in width or length.

2 If the pattern is printed in several sizes, cut carefully along the cutting lines for the size required, being particularly cautious at armholes and neckline to keep to the correct line. If additional width or length is necessary, you will have to attach extra paper, fixed with adhesive tape.

3 Remember that the pattern already incorporates ease or room for movement; it may also include additional width for style and purpose. For example, a loose-fitting overcoat will include a lot more width added to the basic measurements than will a close-fitting waistcoat. While you may need to increase width if the pattern seems obviously to be rather small for you, do not reduce width at shoulders, waist or hips at this stage because it seems too large. It is usually better to do this at the fitting stage.

4 The grainlines must be kept straight and in one continuous line (see fig. 47).

Any pieces of pattern which are not required should be returned to the envelope. You may discover that you need them later on.

Check the following list of measurements on the paper pattern and compare them with your own listed measurements, as in Chapter 8. **Adjust** the paper pattern pieces as, and if, necessary.

Back neck-to-waist length
This will be given on the table at the back

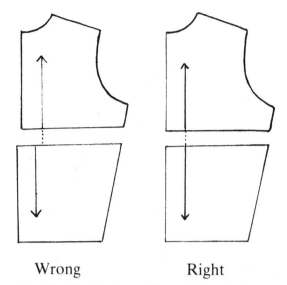

Wrong   Right

Fig. 47 *Keeping the grainline straight and continuous*

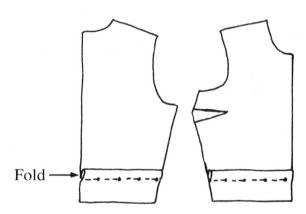

Fold ➤

Fig. 48 *Shortening bodice back and front*

of the pattern envelope, just below the bust, waist and hip measurements for your size.

Adjustments

To shorten, fold a tuck straight across the front and back pieces, between the bust line and the waist, at right angles to the C.F. and C.B. lines (see fig. 48). This folded tuck must be half as deep as the amount you need to remove. Beware of removing too much length; it may be safer to adjust at the fitting stage (pp. 105–6).

To lengthen, draw a line across the front and back pieces, between armhole and waist, at right angles to the C.F. and C.B. lines. Cut on these lines and stick or pin the pieces to paper, so that the gap between them is exactly the extra length you need to add. Check that the gap is level by measuring at each end, and that the grainlines can be rejoined in continuous straight lines (see fig. 49).

Remember to alter similarly all the pieces involved in the top half of the design (excluding sleeves, yoke, collar etc.), including any front facings.

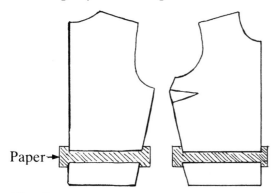

Fig. 49 *Lengthening bodice back and front*

Skirt length
Measure from waistline to hemline, down the C.B., and compare with your own.
Adjustments
To shorten, measure up, from the lower edge of the skirt pattern, the amount which needs to be deducted, then draw in a new cutting line which follows the same curve as the original (see fig. 50(a)). Beware of shortening too much, in case the skirt needs to be lifted at the waistline at the fitting stage.

To lengthen, extend the vertical cutting lines of the skirt pattern to the length required. Add the same extra depth to the lower edge of the skirt pattern all round, so that you have a new cutting line which follows the same curve as the original (see fig. 50(b)).

Sleeve length
Measure the sleeve pattern from the top centre dot to elbow level (where a dart or

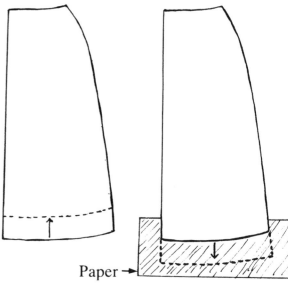

Fig. 50a *Shortening a skirt pattern*

Fig. 50b *Lengthening a skirt pattern*

easing is indicated) and from elbow to wrist (see fig. 51). Check with your own measurements, to ensure that the elbow level is correct.

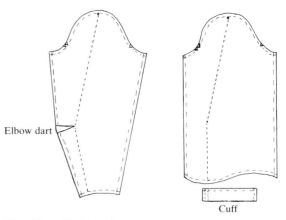

Fig. 51 *Checking sleeve length and elbow level*

Adjustments
You may need to shorten between top and elbow, and lengthen between elbow and wrist, or vice versa; you may need either to shorten or to lengthen both.

To shorten, make horizontal tucks.

74

To lengthen, cut and stick to paper.

For both, use the technique advised for the back neck-to-waist adjustments.

If the sleeve is loose-fitting, with no elbow indication, check its total length against your own, taking into account also the depth of the cuff (if one is included in the design).

Remember to include extra length for blousing in a full sleeve.

Now, by checking with your own measurements, mark on the side seamlines of the paper pattern your own bust, waist, stomach and hip levels (see fig. 52).

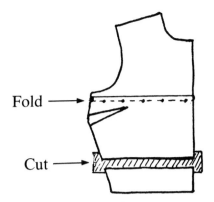

Fig. 53a *Raising the bust dart*

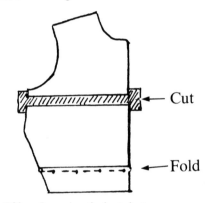

Fig. 53b *Lowering the bust dart*

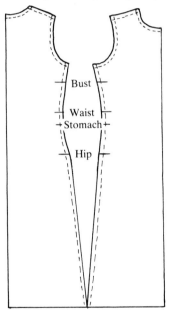

Fig. 52 *Marking bust, waist, stomach and hip levels on side seamlines*

Level of bust dart

Remember that the bust dart should point towards the bust point but should end about 3cm (1¼in.) from it.

Adjustments

To raise, fold a level horizontal tuck, between armhole level and bust level, half as deep as the amount you need to remove. Compensate for this by cutting horizontally between bust level and waist level, and inserting the same depth (see fig. 53(a)).

To lower, cut horizontally between armhole level and bust level, and insert the necessary depth. Compensate for this by folding a level horizontal tuck (half as deep as the amount you have added above the bust) between bust level and waist level (see fig. 53(b)).

Now *re-check* the bust level by fitting the pattern up against your figure, placing the shoulder line and the C.F. line correctly. (The side seamline may or may not lie in the right place at this stage.) The dart from the side seam should now point exactly towards your own bust point. If necessary, readjust the bust-level line.

Now, at the marked bust level, place together any vertical seamlines which come between C.B. and C.F. Take care to avoid the mistake of simply placing one seam allowance upon another.

Note The following checks are for circumference or width measurements. These may not be quite so important if your finished garment will still retain some degree of stretch.

Circumference at bust level
Measure from the C.B. line to the C.F. line and double the resulting figure. Compare this with your own full bust measurement and take into account the amount of extra room necessary for 'ease' and style.

Adjustments

To reduce the circumference, in general, divide the total necessary reduction by the number of vertical seams, then take half this amount off each vertical s.a. *but*, unless the pattern seems very obviously too large, it may be better to leave this until the fitting stage. *Do not remove anything from the C.B. or C.F. lines*, as this would alter the neckline.

To increase the circumference (for figures wearing an A- or B-cup bra), divide the total necessary enlargement by the number of vertical seams, then add half this amount to each vertical s.a. Again, *do not alter the C.B. or C.F. lines*.

(Those who wear a C-, D- or DD-cup bra should refer to pp. 77–9.)

Check and adjust in a similar way the circumference at *waist, stomach and hip levels*.

Back shoulder widths
Measure from the C.B. line to the armhole seamline at the three levels indicated on p. 68 and double the results. The pattern should at least equal your own measurements here, but no extra ease is necessary.

Adjustments

Extend the pattern at the armhole, as necessary, at right angles to the C.B. line (see fig. 54). *Do not reduce* the widths at this stage; this is better done at fitting time (p. 105).

Sleeve width
Measure the pattern from seamline to seamline at (a) underarm level, (b) elbow level, (c) approximately 5cm (2in.) below

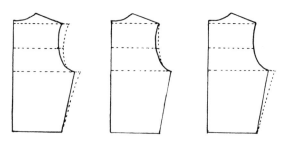

Fig. 54 *Extending back shoulder width at various points*

elbow level, and (d) wrist level. It will not be necessary to check (b) and (c) in the case of a full sleeve. Where there is a cuff or wrist band, check the distance between the fastenings with your wrist circumference measurement.

Adjustments

The sleeve pattern can be cut from top to wrist.

Extra width can then be inserted at the top only, by tapering the insertion to nothing at wrist level (see Fig. 55(a)). If extra width is required all the way down, insert equal width down the entire length (see fig. 55(b)).

Reduce width at the fitting stage.

Fig. 55 *Adding width to a sleeve pattern* **a** *at the top*

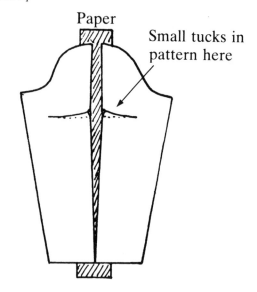

Paper

Small tucks in pattern here

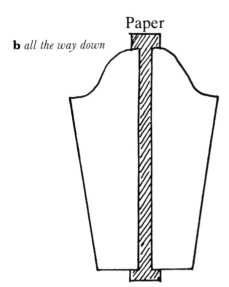

b *all the way down*

Paper

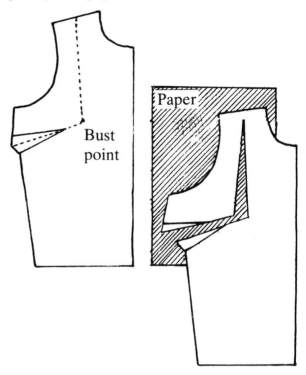

Fig. 56a *Dotted line indicates where to cut the pattern for enlarging the bust dart*

Bust point

Paper

Fig. 56b *Spreading the pattern to give extra width at bust level*

Bust adjustments

For those who wear a C-, D- or DD-cup bra, the following alterations will ensure a better fit, whether or not the pattern already has a bust dart marked.

With a bust dart

Having checked, and adjusted if necessary, the bust level line, check this again by holding the pattern piece up against your body. Take care to see that the shoulder line and the C.F. line are correctly positioned but disregard, for the moment, how the armhole and side seam lines lie.

1 Mark on the pattern, with a felt-tipped pen, the exact position of your own bust point. Re-adjust the bust dart if necessary, to line up with the bust point. (Remember that the bust dart should point towards the bust point but should end 3cm (1¼in.) from it.)

2 Cut the pattern from the side, up the centre of the dart and on to the bust point. From there, cut again, straight up to a point halfway along the shoulder seamline (see fig. 56(a)).

3 Place the pattern on a sheet of plain paper.

4 Open up the cuts so that the gap between the two corners at the bust point is 1.3cm ($\frac{1}{2}$in.) for a C-cup bra; 2cm ($\frac{3}{4}$in.) for a D-cup bra or 3.2cm (1¼in.) for a DD-cup bra.

5 Stick the pattern down (see fig. 56(b)) on to the paper with adhesive tape, taking care to be accurate.

6 Re-draw the dart so that it aims towards the bust point but ends 3cm (1¼in.) short of it. To see how to re-draw the side seam, fold out the dart and turn it downwards. Graduate the cutting-line from the lower line of the dart to the waistline. This adjustment will have widened the original dart and given extra width along the bust line. (As a safety measure, add a further 1cm ($\frac{3}{8}$in.) to the side and C.B. seams; when tacking together for a first fitting, take 2.5cm (1in.) in on these seams, which can then be let out if necessary at the fitting stage.)

7 Check the front-waist length. If necessary, lower the waistline at C.F., curving it up to its present level at the side seam.

With no bust dart

Space for a dart has to be made.

1 *Check and mark* your own bust point on the paper pattern, as on p. 77. Label the bust point BP.

2 With the pattern flat on a table, rule four straight lines (see fig. 57(a)) which all meet at BP:

A–BP from the curve of the armhole.

B–BP slanting upwards from the side.

C–BP from the waistline, parallel with the C.F. line.

D–BP from the C.F. line.

3 Make three cuts from B, C and D to BP.

4 Cut from BP to A only as far as the armhole seamline.

5 On a sheet of firm paper, rule two parallel lines from top to bottom (see fig. 57(b)). The distance between these lines is 1.3cm ($\frac{1}{2}$in.) for a C-cup bra; 2cm ($\frac{3}{4}$in.) for a D-cup bra or 3.2cm ($1\frac{1}{4}$in.) for a DD-cup bra. Label these lines W and X.

6 Rule a third parallel line, Y. The measurement from X to Y is the same as BP to D.

7 Rule a horizontal line at right angles to W, X and Y. Mark BP where this line crosses line X.

8 Place the top half of the pattern on the paper (see fig. 57(c)), matching BP and keeping the C.F. line straight on line Y.

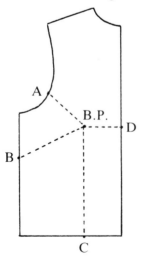

Fig. 57a *Four lines to be marked on pattern, radiating from bust point*

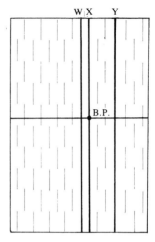

Fig. 57b *Four lines to be drawn on spare paper*

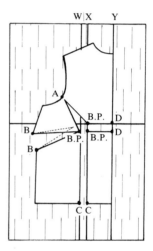

Fig. 57c *Spreading the cut pattern on the paper to give a dart, extra width and extra length*

Spread the cut A–BP open until the BP mark on the lower armhole section touches line W. Tape these in place. A small crease will form in the armhole seam allowance.

9 Place the two lower pieces on the paper, as shown in the diagram: the left side of the line C–BP on line W; the right side of line C–BP on line X, but lowered, so that the waistline is straight. The two lines B–BP must meet at BP, on line W. The space between these two lines is now the dart which will be sewn up when the garment is constructed, but it is, at this stage, wrongly aligned.

10 Redraw the dart, keeping the same width at the wide end but pointing it at BP on line X, and making it end 3cm (1¼in.) short of BP. Fold out the dart and turn it downwards towards the waistline, then cut the paper straight from armhole to waist, down the side cutting-line: this gives the right shape at the wide end of the dart.

The waistline is now bigger, but any necessary adjustment to this can be done at the fitting stage.

It is advisable to try out this alteration on a piece of spare or waste fabric first so that any error can be corrected.

Back adjustments

For those with a rounded back, the following alterations will allow for a better fit from a commercial pattern.

Where more room is required mainly round the C.B. just below the neckline, extra length must be allowed for.

1 Rule a line squarely across the back pattern piece, from C.B. to armhole cutting line, starting at a point approximately 9cm (3½in.) below the neck seamline at C.B. (see fig. 58(a)). Cut along this line. The top part of the pattern now becomes a yoke, so it will eventually be cut on a fold.

2 Add half the extra length required to the yoke at C.B. and the other half to the lower part of the back at C.B. Slope the

Fig. 58 *Adjustments for ' dowager's hump '*
a *Where to cut*
b *Adding extra depth to upper and lower parts*
c *Adding seam allowances*

new seamline to meet the armhole seamline where the ruled line crosses it (see fig. 58(b)).

3 Add 1.5cm (⅝in.) seam allowance to both pieces (see fig. 58(c)).

Note If the top part of the back pattern includes a dart from neckline or shoulder line, draw the dart longer to make it reach the yoke seamline; then fold it out. The bottom of the yoke will now curve up more at the sides to give it the required shape.

When extra room is needed across the shoulder blades, the pattern will need adapting to provide more width as well as length.

1 Rule, and then cut, two lines on the pattern piece. The first is from a point approximately halfway down the armhole, straight across to meet the C.B. line at right angles. The second line runs from *either*

a a point halfway along the shoulder line, *or*

b a point roughly halfway between the neck end of the shoulder seam and C.B. (fig 59(a) and (b)).

Which you choose may depend on the presence of a dart already in one of these positions which can then be enlarged.

If the back is very rounded, a dart (or easing) may be needed in both positions.

Note You cannot make a shoulder dart where the designer has dropped the shoulder seam towards the front of the garment.

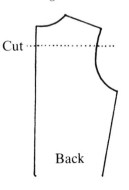

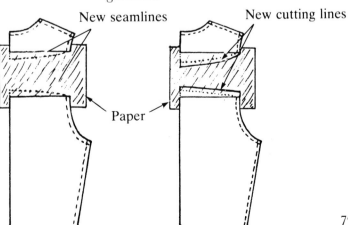

New seamlines   New cutting lines

Cut

Paper

Back

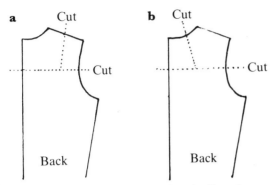

Fig. 59 *Alternative positions of cutting lines for adding extra width as well as depth to the back*

2 Spread the cut pieces as shown (fig. 60(a) and (b)) to form dart space at shoulder or neck, and give extra length down C.B. Keep C.B. line straight. A small pleat will form in the armhole seam allowance.

3 Draw in the dart, making it much shorter and more curved than the cut (fig. 60(c)).

4 If the hump is very pronounced, it is advisable to extend the neck end of the shoulder cutting line inwards, and the C.B. line upwards, by 1–2cm ($\frac{3}{8}$–$\frac{3}{4}$in.), thus giving extra height on the back of the neck. Remember to alter the front shoulder line to match (see fig. 61(a)). This can be adjusted at the fitting stage. Similarly, add a little to the width across the shoulders by drawing a straighter armhole line (fig. 61(b)).

Fig. 60 *Spreading the cut pattern on paper to form dart*

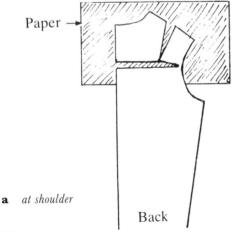

a *at shoulder*

b *at neck, and to give extra length at C.B.*
c *Adjusting the dart*

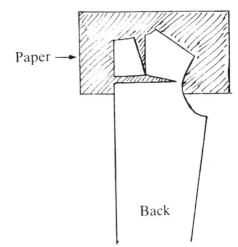

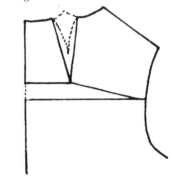

Fig. 61a *Adding extra height at back of neck and extra width across shoulder blades*

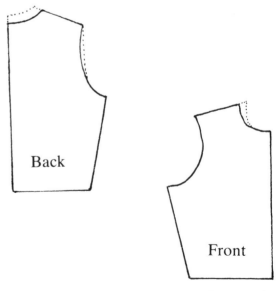

Fig. 61b *Adding extra to front of neckline to match altered neckline at back*

10 Laying out and cutting out

Having prepared the fabric (Chapter 5), checked the pattern measurements and adjusted these if and where necessary (Chapter 9), you are now ready to lay the pattern on your knitted fabric and to cut out.

LAYING OUT

Check through the following list before starting to cut

1 Study the instruction sheets carefully. Make sure that you understand the coding used in the illustrations for indicating right side of fabric (R.S.), wrong side of fabric (W.S.), interfacing, lining etc. Check on how many of each piece you need to cut. (Of course, you may have already knitted some, or all, of the pieces to shape.) Because your knitted fabric is likely to be narrower than the fabric prescribed by the pattern, the layout diagrams will not be of much use to you, but look at the summary of pattern pieces and work out what each one is and where it fits into the whole design.

2 If your cutting-out place is a highly polished dining table or any other smooth, shiny surface, cover it with a thick, closely-woven blanket. This will stop the knitting sliding around and, as it provides a surface to which the knitting can cling, it will help it to stay flat. A checked blanket, giving you straight lines with which you can line up your pattern grainlines, is even better. Obviously, avoid involving the blanket when actually cutting!

3 Make sure that the knitted fabric has had ample time to retract after pressing.

The possibility and degree of retraction will depend on the fibre content of the yarn used and the amount of pressure exerted on the fabric when pressing. Retraction occurring *after* cutting will result in inaccurately shaped and under-sized pieces.

4 Decide which is the R.S. of the knitted fabric. This could be whichever side you find most attractive.

5 Nap. Knitted fabric is more likely to be 'with nap' than woven fabric, i.e. the pieces should all be cut with the top ends pointing in the same direction. This does depend on the stitch pattern, texture and yarn used in the knitting. If in doubt, hang a length of it around your neck so that the two ends hang down on each side of your front: any difference in the two sides should show up. It is probably safer, though often less economical, to cut all the pieces in one direction.

6 The knitted fabric must be straight and flat (see Chapter 5). There should be no bias twist or fluted selvedges. If, despite careful pressing, the selvedges are still wavy-edged, cut the main pieces down the middle of the strip. The side pieces can be used for cuffs, collar bands, belts, waistbands etc., and also for experimenting with the various sewing processes you will be going to use.

7 Mark the grainline of your knitted fabric (with a contrasting coloured thread), up one straight vertical line of stitches, in each length (fig. 62(a)). If you have not placed marker threads at intervals along the selvedges, mark also one or two straight

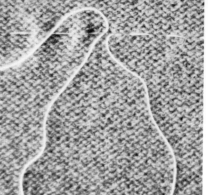

Fig. 62a *Marking the vertical grainline*

Fig. 62b *Marking the horizontal grainline*

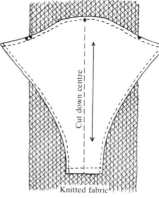
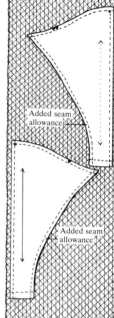

Fig. 63a *Dividing a batwing-sleeve pattern which is too wide for the fabric knitted*

Fig. 63b *The two pieces placed on the fabric for cutting after seam allowances have been added*

rows of knitting, across the width of the fabric (fig. 62(b)). These will not be necessary in cases where the grainlines are obvious because of the stitch pattern used in the knitting.

8 Decide whether you are going to cut through double or single fabric. For example, will you cut both sleeves together, on double fabric placed R.S. together, *or* will you cut each sleeve separately? If cutting separately, *remember* to reverse the pattern when cutting the second sleeve in order to make sure that you have both a left and a right sleeve. In most cases it is safer, as far as keeping the grain straight is concerned, to cut single layers.

9 Some pattern pieces, such as front or neck facings, or inside-pockets, may be better cut from a woven lining fabric rather than from the knit. This reduces the problem of excessive bulk in the finished garment and also stabilises the knitting at these points.

10 Some pattern pieces may be too wide to fit on your knitted fabric. In this case, extra seams will have to be designed. They cannot be hidden, so place them so that they look as if they were part of the original design. For example, a bat-wing sleeve pattern can be sliced down the middle so that a seam runs down the outside of the arm (fig. 63(a)). Skirt pieces can usually be divided up similarly.

Note Remember to add s.a.'s where you have divided a pattern piece, otherwise your garment may be too small (fig. 63(b)).

11 Match the pattern of your knitted fabric (e.g. where horizontal stripes are used) on the vertical seam lines. On the pattern pieces you will find notches on the cutting lines, which indicate that two pieces are to be seamed together. When placing the pattern pieces on the knit, ensure that the same part of the knitted pattern lines up with each of the notches to be paired. For example, on a knit which consists of horizontal bands of navy, emerald and white, if the notch on the side seam of the pattern piece for the garment front lies on a white stripe, then the matching notch on the pattern piece for the garment back must also lie on a white stripe.

12 Plenty of glass topped pins should be used to hold the pattern firmly in place, especially around curves and awkward corners.

CUTTING OUT

Use sharp scissors which are sufficiently strong to do the job efficiently. Struggling with blunt, too-small scissors will only produce fraying problems and will also lead to inaccurate cutting. Try not to lift the fabric more than necessary: slide the scissors along the table top as you cut.

Do be accurate when cutting. Cut exactly down the centre of the pattern cutting-line, or any line you have drawn when adjusting the pattern. The professional pattern-cutters and graders have drawn their lines, calculated to the nearest 1mm ($\frac{1}{25}$in.), and so any adding or subtracting you may do, by careless cutting, will cause problems later when assembling the pieces of your garment.

A note of reassurance here for the faint-hearted: the knitting will *not* immediately disintegrate as soon as it is cut! The pieces should, however, be handled gently and sensibly.

Problems of unravelling

These are rare, except where the yarn used for knitting is very smooth and silky, and the stitch used has gaps in it (as in lace) or the tension is very loose.

In such cases, use the following procedure:

1 Allow extra s.a. when cutting—say 2.5cm (1in.) seams instead of 1.5cm ($\frac{5}{8}$in.).
2 After cutting, move the pins (which attached the paper pattern to the knitting within the s.a.) slightly further in from the edges.
3 Fold in the s.a.'s on the paper pattern so that the 2.5cm (1in.) s.a. on the knitting is exposed. Do this on each cut edge where a seam will come.
4 Cut 6mm ($\frac{1}{4}$in.) wide strips of Vilene Supershape lightweight fusible interfacing. These should be straight (with the vertical grain of the Vilene) for straight edges and following the appropriate curve for neck and armhole edges.
5 Very carefully, carry the cut pieces to the ironing-board. Using a thin, damp pressing-cloth and a sufficiently hot iron, fuse the Vilene strips to the extreme outer edges of each piece where required (see fig. 64). Be very careful not to stretch the edges whilst doing this; press lightly, with an up-and-down motion, until the cloth is dry.
6 The Vilene-secured edges will usually be trimmed off during the construction of

the garment. However, where a flat, open seam is used, they could be left on with advantage, providing they are not visible on the R.S.

After cutting out

Sort out those pieces which require inter-facing or mounting. Remove the paper pattern from them, carry out the inter-facing or mounting processes, replace the paper pattern (fitting it exactly in place) and secure it with a few pins. Leave all the pattern pieces in place, ready for trans-ferring the pattern marks to the fabric (see Chapter 11).

Sort through your waste pieces. Discard the very small strips, but save the rest for use when experimenting with interfacings, machine-stitching, methods of seaming, edge-finishing etc. Scraps are useful, too, for any future alterations to the garment and for repairs, so keep some, if possible, for as long as you keep the garment itself.

Those who make stuffed toys will find left-overs of knitted fabric very useful, both for cutting component parts and for stuff-ing. If and when you really need to clear out a collection of knitted scraps, donate them to the craft teacher at your local school, where they can be used for collages, bean bags etc.

Fig. 64 *Narrow strips of Vilene Supershape lightweight pressed to edges of cut pieces when fraying seems likely*

11 Transferring pattern markings to fabrics

My interpretation of cut-and-sew is simply the use of dressmaking methods on knitted fabrics, and in dressmaking the necessity for absolute accuracy cannot be over-emphasised. Remember that the paper pattern has been drafted so that each mark is correctly positioned to the nearest 1mm ($\frac{1}{25}$in.), so any inaccuracy on your part is going to make the assembly of the pieces much more difficult. Imagine the effect of chipping bits off some of the pieces of a jigsaw puzzle, and adding bits to the others.

All marks on the paper pattern mean something which you need to know in order to be able to assemble the garment correctly. If you are not already an experienced dressmaker, you will need to read the pattern instructions carefully to be sure of what each mark means.

When cutting out is finished, start to mark the fabric with the following points in mind.

1 Decide which pieces, if any, are going to be interfaced. Fuse the interfacings to their knitted counterparts before starting to mark. Marking on the interfacing fabric is usually considerably easier than marking on the knitted fabric. This also applies when knitted fabric is mounted on a woven underlining fabric.

2 Decide on the most suitable marking method (p. 13). You may have to use more than one method on any one garment: e.g. where marks are to be made on the inter-facing, use a sharp soft lead or coloured pencil, or a special marking pen containing water-soluble ink, such as the Pikaby pen.

(Never use an ordinary ballpoint or felt-tipped pen, which may contain ink that will stain the fabric.) The pencil must be newly sharpened so that only a very small mark is made with greater accuracy; a large, heavy mark can spread over 5mm ($\frac{1}{5}$in.) and is therefore too vague. The Pikaby pen needs only a very light touch: heavy pressure will blunt the end and make too large a mark.

Any marks which need to be made on the R.S. of the fabric should be made with a needle and brightly contrasting thread. Do this accurately and securely. The tradi-tional tailor-tacking is often not sufficiently secure, in that the thread ends tend to fall out of the knitted fabric. Chalk marking is often too vague and disappears too quickly.

It is a good idea to get into the habit, when using thread-marking, of always using a certain colour for a specific purpose. For example, always use white for marking the C.F. line (you can use yellow when working on white fabric).

3 It may not be necessary to transfer all the marks to the fabric. For example, if you are reasonably experienced with a sewing machine, it is unlikely that you will need to mark seamlines which are almost always 1.5cm ($\frac{5}{8}$in.) from the cut edges. It is actually much better to practise machining exactly this distance from the edges and to build up a kind of mental image of what this gap looks like; alternatively, use some sort of guide on the bed of the machine, set exactly the correct distance from the needle.

4 Some marks are more important than

others and should always be transferred to the fabric. These include:

a C.F. lines.
b Marks indicating darts.
c Notches on cutting lines which indicate seam matching.
d Marks indicating areas where stay-stitching, ease-stitching or gathering are to be used.
e Dots, small circles, large circles, squares or triangles which indicate precise matching of certain points on two, or more, pieces.

Note A useful tip to remember is that it is standard practice for pattern producers to mark the front of an armhole with a single notch and the back of the armhole with a double notch. Bearing this in mind should save you from sewing your right sleeve into your left armhole, a mistake which most of us have made at some time!

5 It is helpful to mark, with a dot, points where one seamline crosses another, e.g. at the neck end of a shoulder seam, where the neck seamline crosses the shoulder seamline. These dots should then be matched carefully when assembling.

6 If your pattern is printed in several sizes you will need to take particular care to ensure that you are marking the correct dot, notch, dart etc. for your size. The possibility of error here is very high, so check and recheck to avoid mistakes. Seamlines are not marked on these patterns, so you will have to work out for yourself exactly where seams cross by measuring 1.5cm ($\frac{5}{8}$in.) inwards from the cutting lines.

To mark interfaced or mounted pieces, place each piece in turn on a hard, flat surface, interfaced or mounted side up. Replace the paper pattern, fitting it exactly in position. Secure with a few pins, placed well clear of any pattern markings.

Mark notches, using a Pikaby pen or a pencil, by lifting the edge of the paper and marking the fabric beneath by drawing a notch. Make sure that the mark is drawn sufficiently far in from the edge so that it will not be totally covered by overlocking before assembly.

Mark dots, circles, squares etc. within the main area of the fabric by rolling the paper back, unpinning where necessary, until the mark is reached (see fig. 65).

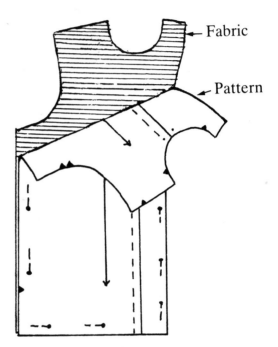

Fig. 65 *Rolling the pattern back so that marks can be made on fabric beneath. Fabric may be the knit alone, or may have interfacing or mounting material attached to it*

To mark lines, such as a C.F. line or a fold-line, fold the paper pattern back exactly along the line, using a few more pins if necessary to hold it in place. Tack-mark a line on the fabric immediately beside the fold in the paper, using the fold as a guide (see fig. 66).

To mark directly on to the knitted fabric follow the same procedure as for interfaced pieces, but use thread-marking if Pikaby pen or pencil marking is difficult or inadequate. Any marks which have to be on the

R.S. of the fabric should also be thread-marked. Careful marking with a Pikaby pen can be made on the R.S., providing that you have tested and proved that it can be completely removed by dabbing with cold water.

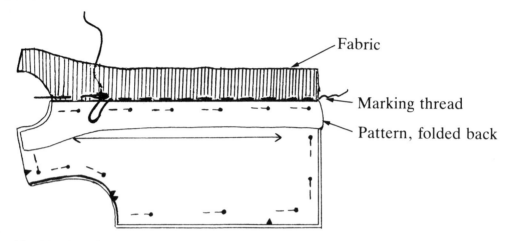

Fig. 66   *Marking a foldline with tacking thread*

12 Sewing up

This chapter is not intended to cover all the possible sewing techniques which can be used in dressmaking. It merely gives advice, where necessary and relevant, on the various stages (roughly in chronological order) in the construction of cut-and-sew clothes, and on the problems likely to be encountered at these stages. The instruction sheets enclosed with your pattern, or a good dressmaking and tailoring text-book (such as *Vogue Sewing*, Ann Ladbury's *Sewing*, or Reader's Digest *Complete Guide to Sewing*) will cover most other aspects.

TERMINOLOGY
Marking and stitching
In order to make sure that you fully understand the terms (as used in commercial pattern instructions and in this book) for methods of holding, marking and stitching, check the following list:

Hand-tacking (or *basting*): sewing two layers of fabric together by means of temporary, fairly long stitches made with a hand needle and thread. This is not recommended on knitted fabrics, except for holding pieces of the garment together when trying on for fitting.

Pin-tacking: pinning two layers of fabric together, *on* the seamline, by means of pins, placed usually at right angles to the seam, i.e. *across* it (see fig. 67).

Machine-tacking: sewing two layers of fabric together by machining with the stitch-length set to its longest point.

Tack-marking: the longest straight stitch on the machine, or hand-tacking, used on

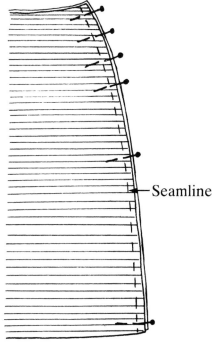

Fig. 67 *Pin-tacking two pieces of fabric together before machining*

one layer of fabric, simply to mark the position of a fold line, a pleat, the C.F. line etc.

Pin-marking: the placing of pins to mark a seamline, or a specific point, such as the end of a dart or the place-marks for a pocket. Only for short-term use.

Stay-stitching: machine-stitching with the stitch length set *very small* ($\frac{1}{2}$ or 1). Usually done with a matching thread, *on* or *almost on* the seamline, to prevent stretching, and also to prevent fraying when the fabric is snipped from the edge to the stay-stitching line, so that the s.a.

Stay-stitching

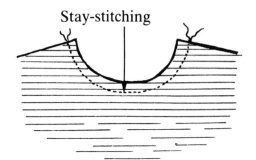

Fig. 68a *Stay-stitching, to prevent fraying when the seam allowance is clipped*

Fig. 68b *Clipped seam allowance*

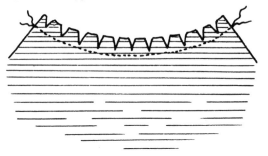

can be spread out (see fig. 68(a) and (b)).

Ease-stitching: two rows of machine-stitching with the stitch length set to its longest point. The underneath threads are then pulled up, in order to reduce the length of the piece of fabric (e.g. the top of a sleeve).

Top-stitching: machine or hand stitching, done on the R.S. of the garment, to decorate or emphasise a seam, the edge of a collar, top of a pocket, etc.

Under-stitching: short length machine-stitching, positioned 3mm ($\frac{1}{8}$in.) from the seamline, which has already joined the facing to the s.a. of the garment; this does not include either the body of the garment itself, or any collar or cuff sewn between the garment and the facing. Used usually on neck and armhole facings (p. 101).

Gathering: as for ease-stitching, but with the underneath threads pulled up more tightly to form gathers in the fabric and to reduce it considerably in length.

Blind-hemming: hand-stitching the hem to a garment, *underneath* the cut and finished edge of the hem, rather loosely and in such a way that the stitching is invisible on the R.S.

'*Stitch-in-the-ditch*': machine-stitching, on the R.S., exactly following, and *in*, a seamline.

Prick-stitch: similar to backstitch, but when the needle has come up from the W.S., it should be re-inserted only a thread or two behind. Most of the sewing thread is then visible only on the W.S., with indentations rather than stitches showing on the R.S.

Fabric layers

The following terms are used for the various layers of fabric which make up a garment. Some are easily confused, so check these also.

Facing: the piece of fabric (or several pieces joined together) cut to fit the edges of a garment and which is attached so as to line these edges, on the inside, e.g. the inside edges of a coat. Facings are often turned to the R.S. to form revers, turn-up cuffs etc.

Interfacing: the woven, non-woven, or knitted fabric which is fused or sewn to the W.S. of the main fabric to give it extra body and firmness. It is usually hidden by facings or linings.

Lining: the matching, toning (possibly contrasting) fabric, cut and sewn to fit inside a garment such as a coat, to give it extra strength or warmth, to hold its shape and to cover up s.a.'s, interfacings etc.

Underlining: a fabric used under light, loosely woven, unstable fabrics, such as chiffon or lace, or very loosely knitted fabrics, to give them support and shape. This is usually done by mounting the fabric pieces on the corresponding under-lining pieces and sewing the two layers together before starting to assemble the garment.

Interlining: a layer of fabric, inserted between the garment and its lining, for extra warmth. Woven 'domette' or the knitted 'Eskimo domette' is usually used for this. Wadding, used for quilting, also comes into this category.

AVOIDING PROBLEMS

Here are some general rules which will help you to avoid cut-and-sew problems

1 Handle your knitted fabrics carefully and with respect. Avoid stretching and pulling which might cause unravelling.

2 Try to anticipate any difficulties you are likely to meet due to the stretch factor in your knitted fabric. Use the appropriate stabilising methods (see Chapter 6).

3 Use only all-polyester (or cotton-wrapped polyester) threads.

4 Do any edge-finishing or overlocking (where seams will be pressed flat and will not be covered by a lining) *before* starting to sew up the garment; it is very much easier at this stage. *Do not*, however, finish edges, such as those of collars and necklines, where the edges will eventually be enclosed within facings. The process of edge-finishing these curved shapes could stretch them out of proportion. Likewise, do not edge-finish armholes where sleeves will later be inserted; it is better to wait until the sleeves have been set in and then to overlock (or bias-bind) the edges of the completed armhole seams. The edge of a hem, being, in most cases, cut *across* the knitting, is very easily stretched in the process of edge-finishing on a sewing machine (a purpose-built overlocking machine does not stretch the fabric edge); so it is better to avoid doing anything to it until after the hem has been trimmed level and is ready for turning up.

5 Always tack-mark the C.F. line unless a seam is positioned there which makes it obvious. This enables you to pin the correct overlap when fitting shirts, coats etc.

6 Whenever you are about to sew two matching pieces of your garment together (e.g. the side seams of a skirt), lay them together flat on a table. Make sure that neither is stretched more than the other, before pinning. Never do this on your lap or with the work held up above the table. If one piece seems definitely longer than the other, check with the paper pattern piece to see which is correct.

7 Pin-tack to hold the fabrics together in preparation for machine-stitching (p. 87 and fig. 67). Hand-tacking (basting) alone is actually a very inefficient method of keeping two layers of fabric together whilst machining. This applies particularly to knitted fabrics, which tend to be more loosely constructed than woven ones. If you really feel it necessary to tack before machining, then leave in the pins, placed across the seamline, removing them just before they go under the presser foot.

For bulky knits, use hairdressers' clips for holding pieces together.

8 Where a seam is particularly difficult to execute (e.g. where a corner has to be exactly matched), use pin-tacking first, followed by small back-stitching by hand, in that particular area. The thread used for this should match the fabric exactly because it should not be necessary to remove these hand-stitches. For additional security, machine exactly over your hand-stitching.

9 Use straight machine-stitching to sew seams which have been completely stabilised by the addition of tape, or where a knitted fabric is sewn to a stable woven fabric.

10 Use a small ZZ stitch ($\frac{1}{2}$ to 1 width) to machine any seams which are likely to stretch.

11 Use a seam-plus-overlock stitch (such as the Bernina 'Vari-overlock') for seams which are required to stretch considerably. If your sewing machine cannot do this, use ZZ stitching set to 2 or $2\frac{1}{2}$ width, and press the seam open flat. If you possess a purpose-built overlocking machine which can trim, seam and overlock in one operation, you have no problem.

12 Plan your sewing programme to include several fittings at appropriate stages. These are rarely mentioned in the instruction sheets included in commercial patterns.

MOUNTING

This is often a necessary process where the knitted fabric is extremely light and unstable.

The purchased fabric used for mounting should be similar in weight but closely woven, e.g. chiffon, organza, crêpe de Chine, etc. The pattern pieces are cut in the knitted fabric, which has previously been pressed and left to relax. Exactly the same pieces are cut again, but this time in the mounting fabric; the corresponding pieces are then placed exactly together (W.S. of the knit against R.S. of the mounting fabric), pinned and machine-tacked all around the edge. From then onwards, the two fabrics are treated as one.

A problem may arise when large areas of knit are mounted (e.g. long flared skirt sections): the knit may not adhere well to the mounting fabric and may actually hang away from it in folds. It is possible, of course, to catch-stitch the knit to the mounting fabric all over each piece, but this is a very time-consuming operation. The answer, in this case, is to mount the smaller pieces used for the bodice area but to make two separate skirts, one of the knit and the other of the mounting fabric, joining them only at the waist seam. (The mounting fabric is thus being used as a lining.) Occasionally it is possible to find a mounting fabric which is suitable for the purpose, but which is slightly fluffy and will therefore give a better grip for the knit, e.g. Viyella, nun's veiling, or even a very fine cotton jersey.

OVERSEWING or OVERLOCKING

Which method you use for neatening the raw edges of s.a.'s, where this is necessary, depends largely on what kind of sewing machine you have and whether or not you have a special, separate domestic overlocking machine.

Sewing machines
A basic ZZ machine can at least do a plain ZZ stitch over the fabric edge (see figs. 13 and 69).
1 Set the zigzag width to its widest point.
2 Set the stitch length to $1–1\frac{1}{2}$.
3 Feed the fabric into the machine so that when the needle swings to the right it descends just off the cut edge, and then pierces the fabric when it swings to the left.

It is possible that this will stretch the knitted fabric on a with-grain edge. It will almost certainly stretch it on an across-grain edge. Always experiment before starting to sew the garment and, if it seems likely that stretching is going to be a problem, try the following measures.
1 Ease-stitch the edge first. Pull up and sew in the thread ends so that the seam edge cannot stretch.
2 If you have a special foot which will guide it, run a thread under the presser

Fig. 69 *Plain zigzag stitch used to oversew raw edges*

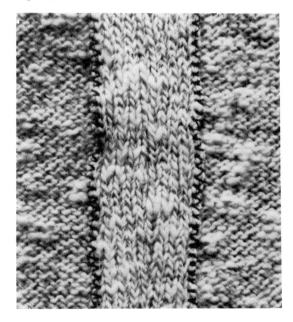

foot, to be straddled by the ZZ stitches and pulled up afterwards.

3 ZZ just *inside* the edge of the fabric (not going over the edge) and then carefully trim off the loose threads of fabric close to the stitching afterwards.

4 Try pressing the stretched edge, pushing *across* it. This will sometimes contract it and will at least flatten it.

More versatile sewing machines can do 3-step ZZ or serpentine stitch (see figs. 14 and 70). This is often better than a plain ZZ for loosely knitted fabrics; it actually sews the fibres together rather than skipping over them. It is also less inclined to stretch the fabric.

Fig. 70 *3-step zigzag, elastic or serpentine stitch used to oversew raw edges*

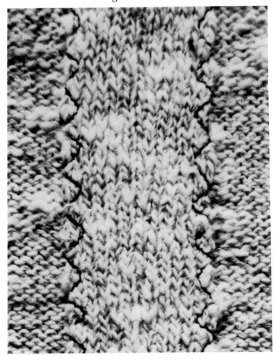

1 Set the ZZ width to its widest point.
2 Set the stitch length to 1.
3 Feed the fabric into the machine so that the last stitch to the right goes off the edge.

Take the same preventive or curative measures to avoid stretching as for basic ZZ machines.

Many modern machines have one or more programmed overlocking stitches, such as the Bernina Vari-overlock, the Husqvarna overlock and the Elna tricot stitch (see figs. 16 and 71). These produce a stitch rather similar to that done by a two-thread domestic overlocking machine, but without trimming, at a slower speed, and still with the risk of stretching the fabric.

Fig. 71 *Vari-overlock stitch, used to oversew raw edges*

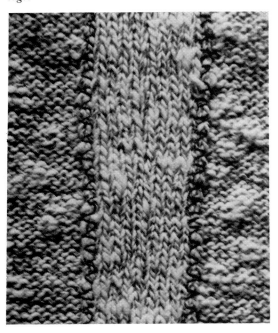

1 Make sure you are using the correct presser foot.
2 Follow the instructions in the manual for setting the stitch width, stitch length, needle position, etc.

Some of the newest machines incorporate a mechanism which actually trims the fabric as well as overlocking it, e.g. the Jones & Brother Compal Ace and Compal Galaxie. This comes nearer to simulating the work done by a domestic overlocking machine. Bernina have produced an accessory which can be attached to most of their machines, which also trims and overlocks. These work very well on woven fabrics, so would be useful when sewing linings; they are satisfactory, too, for trimming, seaming and overlocking finely-knitted fabrics, in one operation. Thicker knits tend to get snarled up and you still have problems with stretching. Again:

1 Use the correct presser foot.
2 Follow the instructions in the manual.

Overlocking machines

A purpose-built, domestic overlocking machine is really the ideal way of finishing the raw edges on machine-knitted fabrics (see Chapter 3 for more details and hints on how to use). Practice is vital when you are new to these machines but, once mastered, they are faster, do not stretch the fabric even when sewing across the grain, and are altogether more efficient (see fig. 72).

Fig. 72 *Raw edge of knit trimmed and overlocked by a domestic overlocker*

SUITABLE SEAMS

Note Stabilised seams can be machined with st. stit. Seams required to be stretched should be machined with a narrow ZZ.

Plain seams
Flat seam

a Seam machine-stitched (ZZ or st. stit.), the full s.a.'s retained and pressed flat on the W.S. The raw edges left unfinished, *or* oversewn/overlocked, *or* bound with narrow bias strips of thin woven fabric (see fig. 73). Top-stitching, on both sides of the seamline, can be done on the R.S. if required, using st. stit. or serpentine stitch (see fig. 74).

Fig. 73 *Raw edge of knit bound with bias strips of woven fabric*

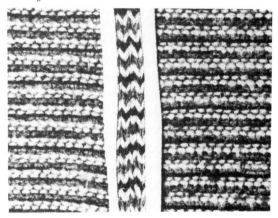

Fig. 74 *Seam top-stitched on R.S. using 3-step zigzag*

b Seam stitched and pressed flat on the R.S., the s.a.'s trimmed, pressed flat and covered with braid or folded bias strip (see fig. 75(a) and (b)).

Fig. 75a *Seam on R.S. being covered by braid which is top-stitched in place (seam allowances have been trimmed)*

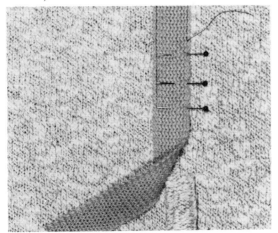

Fig. 75b *The completed seam showing W.S.*

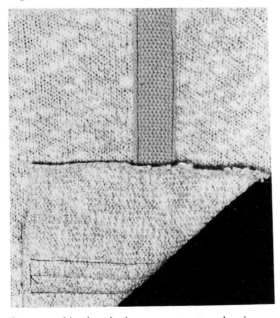

Seam machined and edges oversewn together in one operation. The trimming can be done before, during or after stitching (p. 26; figs. 16, 22 and 76). The finished seam is usually pressed towards the front of the garment,

Fig. 76 *Seam machined and edges oversewn in one operation, by a domestic overlocker*

on the W.S. Top-stitching, parallel with the seamline, can be done on the R.S. if required.

Taped seam. Pre-shrunk narrow tape applied to one of the fabric pieces, along the seamline before machining the seam (see fig. 37).

Felled seam. On the W.S., one of the s.a.'s is trimmed and the other pressed over it. The raw edge of the latter can be oversewn and held in place by top-stitching 1–1.5cm ($\frac{3}{8}$–$\frac{5}{8}$ in.) from the seamline on the R.S. (see fig. 77(a) and (b)). Alternatively, it can be hemmed by hand on the W.S. but this looks less professional.

Decorative seams
Try also some of the decorative seams— piped (or *corded*) (fig. 9), *faggoted*, or *slot* seams. Ricrac braid centred on the seamline of one piece of fabric before seaming to the other makes a very attractive seam (see fig. 10).

93

Fig. 77 *Felled seam*
a *on W.S.*

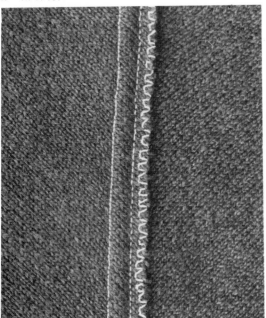

b *on R.S.*

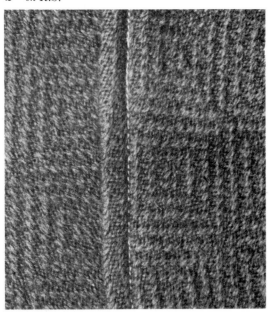

Successful seaming, whether plain or decorative, depends largely on the accuracy with which the pieces are placed together, and on confidence, combined with precision, when machining. *Practice is vital.*

FINISHING GARMENT EDGES

Particular care has to be taken with the edges of cut-and-sew clothes because they are so likely to stretch out of shape. Some form of stabilising, by adding interfacing or a woven fabric, is usually advisable.

Here are some suggestions; use your imagination to think of others.

Facings

These are cut from knitted or woven fabric, stabilised and made firm by the addition of a fusible interfacing (p. 98). A decorative finish can be produced by inserting piping, ricrac braid, lace or frills, between the garment and the facing (see figs. 78, 79(a) and (b)).

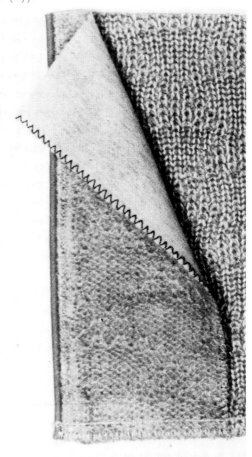

Fig. 78 *Facing cut from knit, interfaced with Vilene Supershape, and with piping in the seamline*

Fig. 79a *R.S. of knit, faced with woven fabric, with ricrac braid in the seamline*

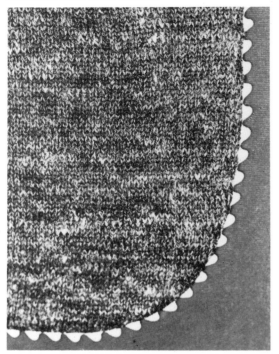

Fig. 79b *W.S. of knit*

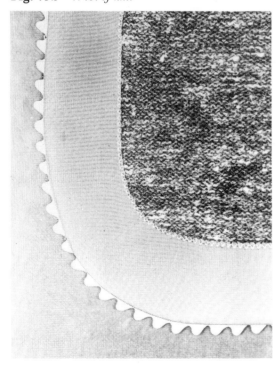

Bindings

1 Bias-cut strips of woven fabric (figs. 80 and 81).

Fig. 80 *Edge bound with bias strips of cotton gingham*

Fig. 81 *Close-up of colour photograph on back cover. Edges bound with bias-cut strips of corduroy to match skirt; jacket fastened with Norwegian pewter clasps*

Fig. 82 *Close-up of colour photograph opp. p. 96. Jacket front edges bound with straight-cut strips of knit fabric. Note the tucks taken in the sleeves to disguise a* miscalculation in length and which have become an attractive addition to the whole!

2 Bias-cut strips of knitted fabric.
3 Strips knitted on the bias to the required width (fig. 24(a) and (b)).
4 Strips knitted straight (plain or ribbed) to the required width, or cut from a wider knit (fig. 82).
5 Purchased (flexible) knitted or woven braid (figs. 8 and 83).
6 Straight-cut strips of woven fabric (fig. 39).
7 Straight woven ribbon, plain or embroidered (fig. 84).
8 Leather or suede strips—or simulated leather/suede.

Ribbons

Ribbon (corded or petersham), applied to the R.S. and then turned to become a flat facing on the W.S., makes a firm edge on which to make machined buttonholes. Use this only on straight edges (see fig. 7(a) and (b)).

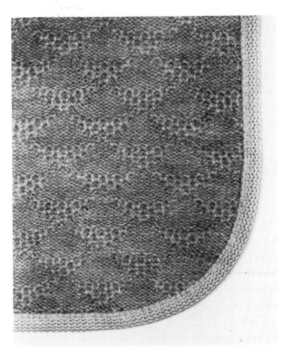

Fig. 83 *Edge bound with purchased flexible braid*

96

Jacket — two different fabrics are used — one hand–knitted in a wool/mohair/acrylic yarn, random dyed in shades of turquoise, pink, lavender and blue; the other machine–knitted in acrylic yarn in marled blue and turquoise. The latter was used for the lower part of the tucked sleeves, the binding, tie ends and the pockets, which are lined. The garment was designed by the author.

Dress and jacket — made from bright courtelle, machine–knitted, combined with linen/polyester woven fabric used for the piping, facings,. bands on the jacket, jacket lining and the cummerbund tie belt. The dress is from a Very Easy Vogue pattern; the jacket was designed by the author. Non-sew snap fasteners are used for the jacket.

Short jacket with matching skirt — knitted in 1 strand of acrylic bouclé and 1 strand acrylic 2/30, plated; plain knitting used on the purl side. The jacket is from a Very Easy Vogue pattern; the skirt was designed by the author. The jacket fabric is totally interfaced with Vilene Supershape medium weight, and lined with polyester lining fabric. Antique buttons are at the neck and cuffs.

Fig. 84 *Two layers of lightweight knit enclosing a layer of polyester wadding, quilted, the edges bound with folded silk ribbon (Michael Chevis, Midhurst)*

Embroidered ribbon, applied to the W.S. and then turned completely to the R.S., makes a decorative edge (see fig. 85). This is best on straight edges but can be induced to cover curved edges with a certain amount of skill and patience.

Hems
This form of finishing is for the lower edges of coats, jackets, dresses etc., and for the ends of sleeves. Tailored garments should include some interfacing in these hems. The raw edge of the hem should not be turned under but should be overlocked, bias-bound or be covered with stretch lace machined on with a small ZZ stitch. Use blind-hemming, by hand or by machine, just *under* the edge of the hem, to attach it to the garment; keep this stitching rather slack (pp. 110–1).

Fig. 85 *Edge faced on the R.S. with embroidered ribbon*

FACINGS (*see definition on p. 88*)

Facings are an important factor in the construction of most garments because they give the necessary strength, firmness and neat finish to the edges. In the case of cut-and-sew clothes, facings also provide the necessary stability which keeps the edges properly shaped and which prevents stretching.

Forms

1 Facings cut exactly to fit the edge of the garment can be cut from the knitted fabric used for the main part of the garment, or from a woven fabric which matches, tones or contrasts. In either case, added interfacings is required. The grainline of each facing piece is matched to the grainline of the garment piece to which it is attached (see figs. 30, 78 and 79).

2 Facings can also be cut in one with the garment piece and then turned to the inside (see fig. 86). Added interfacing is required.

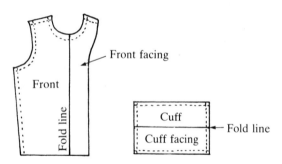

Fig. 86 *Examples of facings cut in one with the corresponding garment piece*

3 For facings for straight edges, such as jacket fronts, sleeve hems etc. ribbon can be used (see fig. 7(a) and (b)), or straight strips cut from a lining fabric. Use interfacing in the latter case.

4 Facings can be cut to fit a whole pattern piece such as a collar, cuff, pocket etc. The knit used for the main part of the garment can be used for these, providing it is not too bulky. In the majority of cut-and-sew situations, however, I find it best to cut these

facings from a woven lining fabric. Interfacing is usually required.

5 Bias facings, strips cut on the bias from woven lining fabric, can be applied to the R.S. of curved edges such as necklines or armholes. These are pinned and machine-stitched, then turned completely to the W.S.; the raw edge is turned in and hemmed, slip-stitched or machined in position. Care and practice is needed to get the right amount of tension or ease on the bias strip, depending on the curve being faced.

If you are using a commercial pattern, the correctly shaped pattern pieces for the facings will have been included in it. If, however, you have either changed the style of a pattern or you are designing your own, you will have to draw the necessary facing patterns yourself.

Preparing and applying facings

Here are instructions for drawing, cutting and applying facings to a plain bodice shape, split up the front in order to be worn as a jacket or coat. Do take great care to be accurate when doing this.

1 (Fig. 87) Lay the knitted front section flat on paper spread on a table. The knit must not be stretched. The vertical C.F. edge must be parallel to the edge of the table, and the lower edge must be parallel with the adjacent table edge. Pull and re-press the piece if necessary, allowing the fabric to cool before proceeding.

Trace shoulder, neck and front edges on to the paper as shown.

The front edge must be a straight line from C to D, drawn with a ruler. A–B and D–E both measure 7cm ($2\frac{3}{4}$in.).

2 (Fig. 88) Remove knitted piece.

Draw another line from A to E, 7cm ($2\frac{3}{4}$in.) inside the first line, as shown.

Add 1.5cm ($\frac{5}{8}$in.) s.a. above A–B and below D–E.

This is now your paper pattern for the front facings.

Mark the straight grainline parallel with

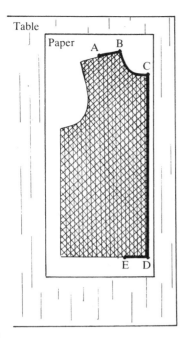

Fig. 87

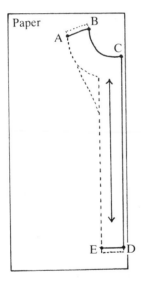

Fig. 88

C–D. Straighten the sharp corner as shown.
Cut around the outer lines.

3 (Fig. 89) Fold the knitted back section along a straight line down C.B., matching neck, shoulder seam, armhole and lower edges.

Pin these to hold them in place. Be careful not to stretch the neck edge.

Place on paper as shown; trace W–X–Y.

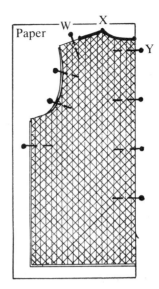

Fig. 89

4 (Fig. 90) Remove the knitted piece.
Draw another line from W to Z, 7cm ($2\frac{3}{4}$ in.) inside the first line as shown.
Add 1.5cm ($\frac{5}{8}$in.) s.a. above W–X as shown.
This is now your paper pattern for half of the back neck facing.
The straight grainline will be on line Y–Z, which will be placed on a fold of the fabric.
Cut around the outer lines.

If the shoulder seams of the garment have not already been machined, do this now. Press the seam open flat.

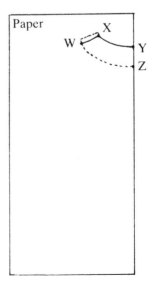

Fig. 90

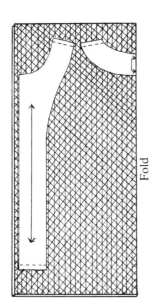

Fig. 91

5 (Fig. 91) Place the pattern pieces for the facings on the fabric to be cut, as shown.

Check that the grainline of the fabric is parallel with those marked on the pattern pieces.

Remember that the centre of the back neck facing must be placed on a fold.

6 Pin firmly in place and then cut out.

Repeat this with fusible interfacing, following the same grainlines.

Press interfacing pieces to W.S. of facing pieces.

7 (Fig. 92) With R.S. tog. join the shoulder seams of the facings, as shown.

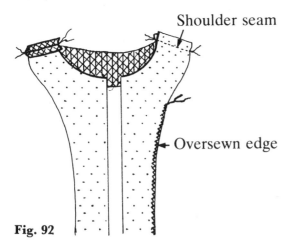

Shoulder seam

Oversewn edge

Fig. 92

Press the seams open flat. Trim back the s.a.'s if necessary.

Machine-finish (using a wide ZZ on a fairly short stitch length) the outer edge of the entire facing.

8 (Fig. 93a) Keeping the work flat on the table, place the completed facing on the garment, R.S. tog., matching shoulder seams, C.B. neck, front corners and lower edges of fronts.

Pin carefully, using plenty of pins placed across the seamline as shown.

Fig. 93a

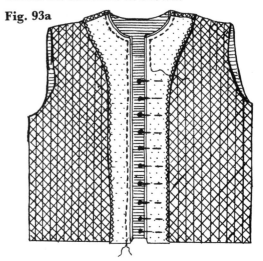

Enlarged detail

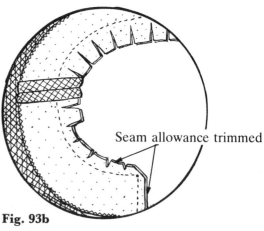

Seam allowance trimmed

Fig. 93b

Machine-stitch, using a short st. stit. (to prevent fraying after clipping or trimming). Clip almost up to the seamline (fig. 93(b)) all around the concave curve of the neck.

This clipping is vital because the facing will not turn properly to the inside and lie flat unless the s.a.'s can spread out to follow the curved shape of the neck. The sharper the curve, the more clips are necessary; the tight curve of a child's neckline might need a clip for every 5mm ($\frac{1}{4}$in.) if the facing is tightly woven.

Trim s.a.'s, leaving at least 6mm ($\frac{1}{4}$in.), except at the top corners which should be cut off diagonally, very close to the stitching.

9 (Fig. 94) Understitch the facing to the s.a.'s.

To do this, lift up the facing, spreading it out as flat as possible (R.S. up), and machine-stitch through the facing and the s.a.'s keeping an even 3mm ($\frac{1}{8}$in.) from the neck seamline.

Follow the curved shape of the facing, so that the clippings underneath are well spread out. Keep the main body of the garment well out of the way.

This process of understitching ensures that the facing stays rolled to the W.S.

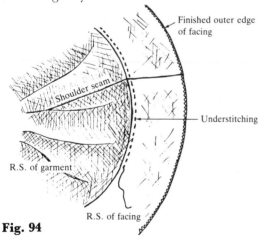

Fig. 94

Note You will find it impossible to carry the understitching right into the corners at the top of the front opening. Stop just before the corner and start again, as near as possible, after the corner.

10 With the facing turned to the W.S. of the garment, pin the shoulder seams of the garment and facing together and secure by hand-stitching *into* (and *along*) the seamline on the R.S. This *can* be done by machine and is known as 'stitching-in-the-ditch'.

I have described these processes in some detail because they can then be used, with adaptations, for a variety of different shapes. For example, following the same guidelines, a simple round neckline with a zipped opening at the back can be faced, or just the straight front edges can be faced and the neckline edged with braid.

The neckline itself could be large enough to go over the head with no opening at all, and the shape can be varied endlessly: V-neck, U-shaped neck, square neck, etc.

A collar can be added, sandwiched between the neck of the garment and the facing, and kept out of the way, with the main body of the garment, when understitching.

Armholes in sleeveless garments can be faced in the same way.

The lower edges of bell-shaped or the medieval type of sleeve can be faced with toning or contrasting fabric which is intended to be seen.

Be careful not to use understitching (which stops the facings rolling to the outside) in a situation where the facing is intended to roll to R.S., e.g. where combined neck and front facings turn back to form revers. In such a case, stop the understitching at a point slightly forward of the shoulder seamline.

Remember to use pre-shrunk tape in the back-neck seamline if both garment and facing still retain a degree of stretch; otherwise you will have a stretched-out back-neck seamline! If the design includes a collar and this has been completely stabilised, it will effectively stabilise the back-neck seamline when attached.

NECKLINES

There are innumerable dressmaking and tailoring methods of finishing necklines. Simply look at any pattern catalogue for ideas and designs, and a good sewing text-book for methods of construction. Any kind of neckline can be adapted for use with knitted fabrics by the judicious use of stabilising methods.

What machine-knitters usually mean by a 'cut-and-sew neckline' has been well covered by the writers of machine-knitting text-books, such as Mary Weaver and Kathleen Kinder, but here are two items which could be helpful. The first, for which I am indebted to Dorothy Gill of London, ensures symmetrical shaping and could lead to the second, which is purely a dress-making method of making a neckband.

Specially knitted neckband

We all know the difficulty of making *quite* sure that both sides of a neck opening are precisely the same, especially when working double-bed Fair Isle. Here is a foolproof way for use on the Passap, but there is no reason why a similar method should not be used when knitting on other machines with ribbing attachments. The method has already been published elsewhere (Kinder, Resource Books) but perhaps this will reach people who have not seen them yet.

For the purpose of this exercise, the standard double-bed bird's-eye Fair Isle is used, but it can also be used with others that have 'N' on the back bed, when BX would be used instead (with pushers, of course). It can also be used whether knitting from a written pattern, using a charting device, or the Form Computer, so it is truly versatile.

Let us suppose our pattern tells us to cast off the centre 16 stitches, followed by the sentence: ' -8, -6, -2×4, $-5 \times 2 \bullet 4R''$ at the neck edge'.

Do not cast off, but, at the start of the neck division, put the centre eight stitches from the front bed to the corresponding

Fig. 95 *A symmetrical neckline marked in the knitting process*

needles of the back bed, and put into neutral position the empty needles and unnecessary pushers on the front bed. Change to black strippers and knit four rows. Next, at either side of the neck, transfer four stitches to the corresponding back bed needles (i.e. half of the eight detailed in the instructions). Knit four rows, then follow by transferring three at each side (half of six) followed by two twice and one five times, each time putting away the pushers and knitting four rows. The back bed continues to knit an alternate needle slip-stitch, while on the front, the outline of the neck shaping is made clear and precise. However complicated the design, it will be exactly the same at both sides (see fig. 95).

After casting off, work a line of firm elastic stay-stitches round this outline, either by hand or with a sewing machine.* Stitch one or both shoulder seams, as convenient, then stitch by stitch, through the open loops of your border, attach it in the usual manner on the outside, just covering the outline you have made. Cut away the single bed section in the centre, close to the elastic stay-stitches, and attach the inside of the neck border, thus enclosing the cut edge.

Vee, square and U-shaped necks can be treated in the same way.

T-shirt neckline (Fig. 96)

The second method is one which has been used by manufacturers of knitwear at the cheaper end of the market for a very long time. The end result is, to be honest, not as attractive in appearance as the specially knitted neckband which encloses the cut neck edge completely, and is attached by hand-sewing. It is, however, a perfectly acceptable and much quicker method of finishing a neckline on casual clothes such as track suits and T-shirts; also for babies' and children's wear. Those dressmakers who are not also machine-knitters find this useful.

I assume here that the body of the garment has been knitted straight up to

shoulder level and then cast off in a straight line.

Note Dorothy Gill's method of ensuring that the neckline is absolutely symmetrical (up to *) could be used instead of (1).

1 Having joined the shoulder seams, try the garment on and look at it in a mirror. Decide exactly where the neckline is going to be on the garment, and mark it all the way round, using a marking pen, pencil, pins or contrasting thread. Take care to see that the two halves, on either side of the centre line, are evenly marked.

2 Measure the neckline by standing the tape measure on its edge actually *on* the seamline, curving it to follow the seamline as you go. Be very accurate about this.

3 Cut the neckband. This will be an absolutely straight strip of knitted fabric cut *across* the width of the knitting. (Take care to cut straight along one row.) The *width* of this strip will be approximately 9cm ($3\frac{1}{2}$in.) and *its length will be about three-quarters of the length of the measured neck seamline*. It is unlikely to need more length, but could require a little less if the knit is very stretchy.

4 Fold this neckband in half lengthwise, and press the fold lightly. Try not to stretch it. If it does stretch, measure it again and cut off the extra length.

5 Stitch the ends of the strip together to form a circle; then re-fold it along the previously pressed line. The s.a.'s should now be hidden, inside the fold.

6 Decide whether the seam in the neckband will come at C.B. or at the left side. Then mark C.B. and C.F. on the band. Mark two more points halfway between these, thus dividing the band into equal quarters. Divide again into eighths.

7 Cut out the neck shape of the garment, allowing a 1.5cm ($\frac{5}{8}$in.) s.a. outside the marked neckline. If the danger of fraying seems great, then machine a line of ease-stitching along the seamline; if this stretches the neckline a little, pull up on the bobbin

thread to put it back to the right size, and make another machined line in exactly the same place but on a medium stitchlength. These lines of stitching will undoubtedly snap the first time the neck is pulled over the head (unless the neck hole is very large), but by that time the neck-band will have been attached, so no harm will ensue.

8 Mark the neckline of the garment at C.B. and C.F. and then divide and mark into eighths, as you did for the neckband.

9 Pin the band to R.S. of the garment, raw edges together, pinning *across* the seam-line, matching up all the marks on neck edge and collar band. *Stitch*, using a narrow ZZ stitch and a medium stitch length, exactly on the seamline.

10 Trim the s.a.'s to approximately 6mm ($\frac{1}{4}$in.) and then overlock the raw edges, stretching them out a little.

11 Press lightly on both the R.S. and the W.S., pressing the seam away from the neck edge.

12 Catch-stitch the neck seam to the shoulder seams on the W.S.

Fig. 96 *T-shirt neckline, seamed and oversewn by sewing machine*

This, basically, is the same method as that used for attaching folded ribbed cuffs to the ends of sleeves or the ankles of track-suit trousers (see figs. 11 and 97). Waist-bands can also be made like this, for the tops of skirts and for the lower edges of sweaters, anoraks etc.

FITTING

Proper fitting, for those who do not conform absolutely to standard sizing, starts with purchasing (or drafting) the pattern in the nearest correct size, followed by the adjustment of that pattern in those areas where the actual body differs from the standard one. From then onwards (except in a few extreme cases), only minor alterations should be needed.

Guidelines

Here are some basic guidelines; for more detailed information, read Natalie Bray's *Dress Fitting*, or *Vogue Sewing*, etc.

1 Before you start, make sure that you are aware of the designer's intentions regarding the style. Is it intended to be a very close-fitting garment or is it meant to be very loose? Or is it somewhere between these extremes?

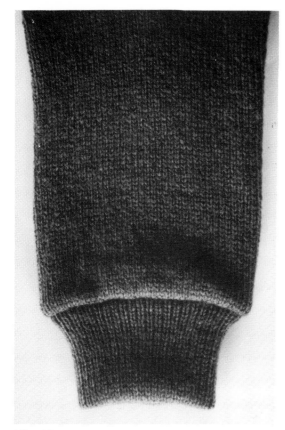

Fig. 97 *Cuff made and attached by same method as the T-shirt neckline*

2 Have fittings at several different stages in the construction of the garment. Use a long mirror in a good light, with a hand-mirror for looking at the back view.

3 Always put the garment on R.S. out, because the two sides of your body are unlikely to be exactly the same.

4 Make sure that the C.F. line is clearly tack-marked. Mark both C.F. lines where the garment opens at the front, and pin these exactly together when fitting.

5 If the garment has a waistline seam, try on the top and bottom halves separately, marking the correct waistline on each before putting them together (see this page for 'tape method').

Check the following, where appropriate, and pin-mark any necessary re-alignment:

1 The position of:

a the waist seamline (see 5 above),

b any dart pointing towards the bust,

c other darts,

d the neckline,

e the armhole seamlines. Check these *after* the neckline is completed and *before* attempting to set in the sleeves (except for raglan shapes). Style is important here, e.g. the tops of puffed sleeves come further in on the shoulder (and extended shoulders further out) than a plain set-in sleeve.

2 For tightness anywhere: horizontal creases indicate this. In cases where the knit still retains a degree of stretch, beware of relying too much on this quality. Let out seams if necessary.

3 For excessive fullness anywhere: remove some if necessary.

4 For any vertical seams which are not hanging straight: lifting at some point may be necessary to correct this.

5 Sleeve length

6 Hem length: a line, level with the floor, must be marked (p. 109).

Bodices and skirts

Use the tape method of marking the waist-line correctly, when fitting bodices and skirts.

On a bodice

1 Put on the bodice. Pin up any front or back opening by pinning the seamlines together or by matching the C.F. or C.B. lines where there is an overlap.

2 Tie a piece of narrow cotton tape tightly around the waist, making sure that it eventually sits exactly where you feel your waist is. The ends of the tape should be tied over the point at which the bodice opens.

3 First pull the bodice tightly down under the tape; then lift it wherever necessary, e.g. to produce blousing above the waist, if that is part of the design. Look in a mirror for this.

4 Pin the tape to the bodice all round,

placing the pins along the middle of the tape and parallel with it.

This line of pins now marks exactly where the waistline seam will come on the bodice.

5 Untie the tape and take off the bodice.

6 If you feel sufficiently confident, cut off any surplus fabric below the tape, leaving a 1.5cm ($\frac{5}{8}$in.) s.a. If you have any doubts, replace the line of pins with a line of tack-marking in a bright colour, and leave the extra fabric in case you later decide to pull up more fullness above the waistline.

On a skirt

1 Put on the skirt. Pin together the top opening, matching the seamlines. Check that the C.F. line is correctly positioned on the body.

2 Tie the tape tightly around the waist, making sure that it sits exactly on your waistline. Tie the ends of the tape over the skirt opening.

3 Pull the skirt up under the tape until just the 1.5cm ($\frac{5}{8}$in.) s.a. is above the tape all round.

4 Look in the mirror at how the seams of the skirt are hanging. Look also at the bottom of the skirt, to see how level it is. If the skirt dips at the front hemline and the bottoms of the side seams tilt towards the back, this indicates a need for pulling up the skirt at the front, above the waist.

If the skirt dips at the back hemline and the bottoms of the side seams tilt towards the front, this indicates a need for pulling up the skirt at the back above the waist.

If the C.B. or C.F. lines (or both) swing to one side, this usually indicates a need to lift the skirt top at the opposite side.

Creases across the C.B. just below the waistline (usually due to a hollow or 'sway' back) indicate the need to lift the skirt above the tape in that area.

5 Pin the tape to the skirt all round, pulling the skirt up where necessary, so that the bottom edge is as level as possible. (This is particularly important when the fabric has large checks or horizontal lines on it.)

The tape now marks exactly where the waistline of the skirt should come.

6 Untie the tape and take off the skirt.

7 Trim off any surplus fabric above the tape, leaving 1.5cm ($\frac{5}{8}$in.) s.a.

The possible causes of skirts hanging unevenly are too numerous to go into here. Figure faults (such as one hip being larger than the other) and how the weight of the body is carried (some people with large tummies tend to lean backwards!) all have an effect. For much more detailed information, consult Natalie Bray's *Dress Fitting*.

Once you have discovered the fitting alterations you need to carry out for your own particular figure faults (and we *all* have some!), you will be able to cope more easily with these at the pattern alteration stage.

LININGS

This is a vast subject on its own, so for general help with the various ways of making and attaching linings you should follow the directions in your dressmaking pattern, or, if you are designing your own, a good dressmaking/tailoring manual will provide most of the answers.

The following hints and suggestions cover some of the areas which, from my experience, require explanation, and which are not always clearly stated in instruction leaflets and manuals.

Skirts

In a cut-and-sew skirt, an attached lining usually improves the look and helps to retain the shape, but you may manage to get away with simply wearing it over a good foundation slip. If the skirt is already interfaced with fusible knitted nylon, an added lining may make it too bulky.

The fabric used for the lining should be reasonably firm and preferably anti-static. The fibre of the lining may depend on the fibre used for the knitting of the skirt fabric, but a woven anti-static nylon or polyester can be satisfactory for most purposes. If you wish to retain a little stretch in the finished garment, try a knitted nylon lining.

A skirt lining should generally be exactly the same shape and size as the skirt to which it is attached, providing it has an opening from the waist downwards towards the hip level. Exclude from the lining any fabric which, in the skirt, is pleated underneath the main part.

For a pull-on skirt, with no opening, the top of both the skirt and the lining must be cut big enough to slip reasonably well over the hips. The top of the skirt, plus its lining, is then attached to an elasticated band which gathers it in to fit the waist. This type of skirt may not suit everyone because of the gathers around the top, but by making the skirt fit the hips quite closely, the gathers can be reduced to a minimum.

It is a sensible precaution to try on the skirt lining on its own, before sewing it in to the skirt. Make sure that it fits well over the hips, but not so tightly that it creases horizontally.

A straight skirt which has a kick-pleat will need a split in the lining to allow room for movement.

In a gathered skirt where the gathering is minimal, cut the lining exactly the same as the skirt. Where there is a lot of gathering, use a plain A-line shape for the lining to avoid excessive bulk at the waistline.

Where the skirt has darts, press the corresponding darts in the lining in the opposite direction, to avoid bulk.

Attaching a skirt lining

1 Machine-tack the lining, W.S. tog., to the top of the skirt, keeping the edges level, matching seams, darts etc. (Do this *after* inserting the zip and protective flap, but *before* attaching the waistband.)

2 Turn in and hem the lining around the zip opening, keeping it well away from the zip teeth.

The lining should otherwise hang separately from the skirt. Because the knitted fabric could stretch in wear, it is unwise to attach the lining to it at the hem.

Hemming the lining

(Do this *after* the skirt hem has been levelled and finished.)

1 Place the skirt, R.S. out, over the ironing-board so that the board is encircled by the skirt.

2 Smooth out the skirt and lining fabrics, matching up the seams. The lining should now project below the finished hem of the skirt.

3 Trim the bottom of the lining to an even distance of 2cm ($\frac{3}{4}$in.) below the edge of the skirt.

4 Turn up and press 2cm ($\frac{3}{4}$in.) all around the lining edge.

5 Turn up and press a further 2.5cm (1in.) around the lining edge.

6 Pin this hem in position, placing the pins *across* the hem.

7 Machine-stitch, using a straight, ZZ or serpentine stitch.

8 Press the hem well.

Jackets and coats

These should be included in your commercial pattern; otherwise you will have to invent your own. The following is a rough guide.

1 Cut sleeve linings on the garment-sleeve pattern.

2 Cut front linings on the garment-front pattern.

3 Cut the back also on the pattern, but allow 2.5cm (1in.) extra at the C.B. line for a long pleat from neck to hem.

4 Cut linings for pockets.

5 Machine-stitch front and back lining pieces together and press seams flat. Do not sew in sleeve linings yet.

6 Pin lining into coat (W.S. tog.) matching seams, underarm points, etc.

7 Pin-mark a line (on the lining fabric only) exactly where it lies on the edge of the coat-facing, from hem to shoulder, and also around the back of the neck if a back-neck facing is there.

8 Remove the lining from the coat. Cut off the front and neck edges keeping exactly 3cm (1¼in.) outside the pin-marked line, following any curves in it.

9 Stay-stitch exactly 1.5cm (⅝in.) from the newly cut edge. Clip any concave curves and then press the 1.5cm (⅝in.) s.a. to the W.S., folding on the stay-stitching line.

10 Re-pin the lining into the coat, matching seamlines etc. as before. The folded outer edges of the lining should now fit exactly 1.5cm (⅝in.) over the edges of the facings.

11 Pin all round and then catch-stitch in place by hand. (To give a couture look, piping can be added to this seam.)

12 Machine-tack the armhole seamlines together.

13 Sew the hem of the lining, either by machine, leaving it to hang separately from the coat hem, or by hand, catching it to the hem of the coat with a tuck downwards to allow for movement.

14 Stitch up the sleeve-lining seam. Ease-stitch the top of the sleeve. Stay-stitch, and clip up to, the under-arm seamline. Press the s.a. to the W.S.

15 Hem the folded seamline of the sleeve lining over the raw edges around the armhole.

16 Hem the lining of the sleeve to the turned-up sleeve end, leaving a small tuck downwards for movement.

Dresses

Consider, first of all, whether a lining is really necessary in a particular dress, or whether it could be better with a well-fitting slip worn under it.

If a lining *is* to be put in, then it should be roughly the same shape (and certainly the same size) as the dress. In the case of a very full, flowing design, however, keep the lining fairly straight and slim-fitting.

In most types of dress, it is best for the lining to be attached only at the neck and armholes, but this may not be practicable for designs which include a waistline seam.

Suitable fabrics are the same as for skirts but can also be lighter in weight.

If the knitted fabric is transparent or lacy, a more expensive fabric such as silk crêpe de Chine or polyester chiffon would probably look better. When considering lining fabrics for see-through knits, do some experimenting with different colours because the colour of the lining can alter dramatically the appearance of the dress fabric. A flesh-coloured lining can give the illusion of nudity under the dress! An emerald-green dress with a turquoise-blue lining will look totally different from the same dress lined with black.

The hem of the lining can be machine-stitched, as for skirt lining hems, and should hang 2.5cm (1in.) above the hem of the dress.

Other types of lining

1 Cotton jersey (purchased) for garments in which you want to retain some of the stretchability of the knitted fabric. The only drawback is that, when used for coats and jackets, it does not slip so easily over other clothing.

2 Showerproof cotton poplin, gabardines and lightweight tweeds, when used as edge-to-edge lining, with a closely knitted fabric, make warm and reversible anoraks, coats and jackets.

3 A cotton-print lining, in a knitted fabric jacket, worn over a dress of the same cotton print.

4 Fur fabric, which can now be purchased in almost any colour, makes a superbly warm jacket or coat. The knit usually clings well to it and is, of course, stabilised by it (see fig. 4).

5 Trousers made of knitted fabric can be lined totally with lining fabric made into a fitted pair of similar trousers, suspended on the inside, from under the waistband.

6 Quilted cotton on the inside of a knitted jacket shape adds firmness and wonderful warmth.

HEMS

Badly finished hems are so often the tell-tale signs which say 'home-made'. It is infinitely worthwhile taking time and trouble to get them right. Hang the garment on a coat-hanger, preferably for several days, before tackling the hem. I am assuming here that the lower edges of the skirt pieces have been *cut* to shape rather than being shaped and given edge-finishing on the knitting machine. In the latter case, any adjustment necessary (where figure and/or posture are less than perfect) to make the skirt hem level with the floor, would have to be done at the *top* of the skirt before attaching a bodice or a waistband.

A level hem

The hem (on a skirt, coat, dress etc.) must be level—with the floor! It is not level if it simply measures the same all round, from waistband to lower edge. The curve of the hips, figure faults, incorrect posture etc., may all have to be taken into account.

The distance upwards from the floor can be measured by a bamboo cane with a rubber band around it (the band is moved up or down as required for different heights) but a proper wooden hem-marker, on a metal tripod stand, with a sliding guide for inserting pins, which can be fastened at the required height, is a valuable investment. Someone else must do the marking, because it is important that the wearer of the garment should stand absolutely still and look straight ahead; otherwise the pin-line cannot be level.

Hem depth

Decide how deep the hem can be and cut it to this level depth below the pin-line all round.

Hems on dresses and skirts can, if desired, be made very narrow. If the raw edge is overlocked first, only 6mm ($\frac{1}{4}$in.) need be turned up and this can then be machined, using ZZ or st. stit.'s. Alternatively, turn up about 1.5–2cm ($\frac{5}{8}$–$\frac{3}{4}$in.) and

make two lines of straight stitching, one close to the fold and the other on the hem edge. This could stretch the hem, so experiment first to check on how it will look.

A deliberately stretched-out hem on a lightweight dress or skirt can actually look very attractive, providing it is very narrow.

Neatening

The raw hem edge now has to be neatened to prevent fraying. As a general rule, it often appears that the less you do to the hem edge, the better. As it is usually *across* the grain of the knit, it is very easily stretched, unless the fabric has been well stabilised beforehand. Use the following guidelines.

1 Never turn in the hem edge, as you would when making a cotton dress, or as you can do when hemming a lining. This creates too much bulk at the top of the hem and is also likely to make it stretch.

2 Preferably overlock the edge with a domestic overlocking machine. This is the neatest and most efficient way of doing it. If your overlocker does a chain-stitch as well as overlocking the edge, thread up the chain-stitch needle, despite the fact that you are not actually making a seam; it will help to prevent stretching.

3 If no overlocker is available, try one of the over-edge stitches on your sewing-machine, preferably with an additional thread placed on the fabric in such a way that the over-edge stitch straddles it. This thread can be pulled up afterwards to contract the stretched edge. You may have a special presser foot designed to guide this extra thread.

4 Stretch lace, 1–2.5cm ($\frac{3}{8}$–1in.) wide, can be machined to the hem edge with a small ZZ stitch (see fig. 6). This must first be pinned in position (with both hem and lace flat and unstretched), keeping the work flat on a table, and the pins *across* the seamline. Experiment with this before trying it on your garment. If, during machining, stretching has occurred, try it again, pinning with a little tension on the elastic lace.

Once the lace is applied, it can be blind-hemmed to the garment, by hand or machine.

Note that the *edge* of the hem should never be sewn to the garment; doing this produces the bump on the R.S. which can ruin the look of the whole garment.

Always do the blind-hemming approximately 6mm ($\frac{1}{4}$in.) *below* the edge of the hem.

Blind-hemming

By hand

To aid understanding, illustrations show a small strip of knit being hemmed, rather than a complete skirt hem.

1 With the W.S. facing you, fold down the hem on the pre-marked fold line. Pin in position, placing the pins parallel with the hem edge (see fig. 98(a)).

2 Fold the hem back until approximately 6mm ($\frac{1}{4}$in.) of the lace-edged or overlocked hem is standing up above the fold (see fig. 98(b)). Pin again in the same way.

3 Remove the first line of pins.

4 Take the needle and thread diagonally from right to left, taking a bite out of the hem edge and then a thread out of the fold, in one movement (see fig. 98(c)).

5 Continue, repeating this diagonal stitch, in a left-to-right direction. Do not pull the thread tight and make no more than four stitches to every 2.5cm (1in.).

By machine

This works very well on most knitted fabrics. Follow the instructions in your machine manual carefully, and make sure you are using the special presser foot provided for blind-hemming.

1 With the W.S. facing you, fold down the hem on the pre-marked fold line. Pin in position, placing the pins parallel with the hem edge, as in fig. 98(a).

2 Fold the hem back until approximately 6mm ($\frac{1}{4}$in.) of the hem is standing up above the fold (see fig. 99(a)). Pin again, but this time place the pins at right angles to the fold.

3 Remove the first line of pins.

4 Place the work under the sewing machine presser foot, with the main part of the garment to the left and the hem edge to the right. The edge of the fold should be up against the guide on the foot. Check that needle position, stitch selector and stitch length are all correctly adjusted for blind-hemming. Set the stitch width to about 3.

5 Turning the fly-wheel by hand, slowly execute the st. stit.'s on the edge of the hem fabric. As the needle starts to swing over to the left to catch in the edge of the fold, you must *stop*. It is at this stage that you must adjust the stitch width! Set it so that when the needle comes down on the left it just catches in a mere thread or two of the fold (see fig. 99(b)).

6 Carry on blind-hemming, taking it slowly at first. Check that you are catching in the fold when the needle swings to the left; adjust the stitch width a fraction if you

Fig. 98a   **Fig. 98b**   **Fig. 98c**

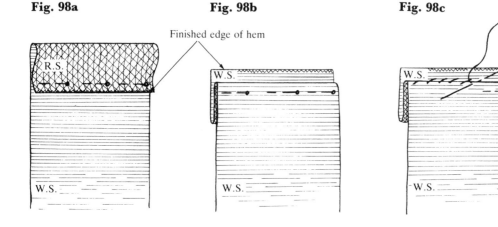

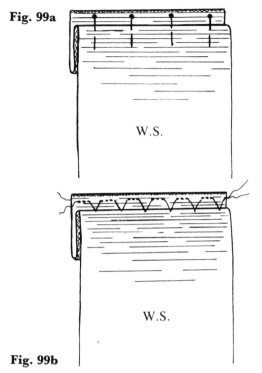

Fig. 99a

W.S.

W.S.

Fig. 99b

are either missing the fold or taking too large a bite in it. Once you are satisfied, carry on, watching carefully to see that the fold is close to the guide on the foot.

Pressing hems

1 Place the garment over the ironing-board, W.S. out. Press upwards from the bottom edge of the skirt to the hem edge. Steam is helpful but not too much pressure. *Never press over the turned-up edge of the hem*: it could make an indentation mark on the R.S.
2 Press downwards from the waistband to just under the edge of the turned-up hem, still on the W.S.
3 Turn the garment to the R.S. and press lightly from the top downwards to the bottom, skating gently over the hem sewing-line.
4 To obtain a sharp crease at the fold-line at the bottom of the skirt, place a damp pressing cloth over the hem area; press quite firmly, taking care not to go over the sewing-line; remove the damp cloth and

immediately bring your pounding-block (p. 11) smartly down on to the fold, and hold it there for several seconds. The combination of heat, moisture and pressure sets the crease firmly, as the untreated wood block absorbs the steam. The use of the back of a clothes brush for this job is not so effective because the wood has usually been polished and is therefore not so absorbent.

Interfacing

Hems on jackets and coats usually need interfacing, to strengthen and stabilise the edges of the garment, in addition to any interfacing already attached to the main body pieces. Use straight strips of Vilene Supershape in a suitable weight, cut on the same grainline as the fabric to which it is to be fused.

The width should be the depth of the hem allowance, plus 2cm ($\frac{3}{4}$in.). Fuse these strips to the W.S. of the main fabric, keeping the edges together. The Vilene will come 2cm ($\frac{3}{4}$in.) over the fold of the hem (see fig. 100).

Fig. 100 *Fusible interfacing applied to hem area*

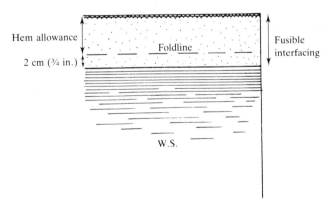

Hem allowance

2 cm (¾ in.)

Foldline

Fusible interfacing

W.S.

FASTENINGS
Buttons and buttonholes

Modern sewing machines have made sewn buttonholes comparatively simple and speedy. Make sure, however, that the fabric in the area of both buttons and holes has

111

been properly and firmly stabilised. Choose button-size by matching the diameter of the button to the width of the overlap (c.f. line to edge).

Vertical buttonholes should lie on the C.F. line with the button positioned just below the top of the hole.

Horizontal buttonholes should lie *at right angles to* the C.F. line, starting 6mm ($\frac{1}{8}$in.) over it towards the edge. This allows room for the button shank when the button is sewn on the C.F. line.

Zips

Zips which are required to be hidden are best applied by the lapped method. They should be firmly pinned in position (pins at right angles to the zip) and then sewn by hand using a prick-stitch. Reinforce, if necessary, by machining over the hand-stitching using a zipper foot on the machine. Take care not to stretch the garment fabric; once the zip is sewn in, the zip tapes stabilise the seam.

For a decorative zip-fastening, use a chunky zip and stitch the fabric around the zip teeth (not over it). This can also be done with the s.a.'s on the R.S., afterwards covering them with applied embroidered ribbon.

Other types

Decorative snap-in fasteners (see p. 18 and fig. 5) should be applied to well-stabilised and strengthened fabric, following the manufacturer's instructions.

Norwegian pewter clasps should be hand-sewn in place (see fig. 81).

Velcro should be pinned and machine-stitched in place, using a st. stit. on the edge or a small ZZ on and off the edge.

Ties can be made with French-knitting cords, or rouleau.

Appendix I

SUPPLIERS AND MANUFACTURERS IN U.K.

(Items marked * are usually available from drapers or haberdashery departments.)

Belts and buttons made to order from own fabric, knitted or woven.

> Harlequin, Lawling House, Manningtree Rd, Sutton, Ipswich, Suffolk IP9 2SW

Buttons*

> The Button Box, 44 Bedford St, London WC2E 9HA
>
> The Warehouse, 39 Neal St, London WC2
>
> Creativity, 15 Downing St, Farnham, Surrey and 35 New Oxford St, London WC1. (Norwegian pewter clasps and buttons. Horn and olive-wood buttons.)

Haberdashery* (general)

> MacCulloch and Wallis Ltd, 25–26 Dering St, London W1R 0BH. Personal or mail-order. Good catalogue.

Interfacings

> George Howe (Textiles) Ltd, 111 Philips Park Rd, Manchester. For fusible knitted nylon tricot ('Easy-knit' in U.S.A.); will send name of nearest stockist; otherwise, try to persuade a local shop to stock this.
>
> MacCulloch and Wallis Ltd, (address above) for large variety of interfacings, including fusible cotton muslin ('Shapewell' in U.S.A.) and fusible knitted nylon.

> Metropolitan Sewing Machines, 321 Ashley Rd, Poole, Dorset BH14 OAP. For fusible knitted nylon.
>
> Vilene* Supershape fusibles: see Vilene

Iron covers

> (Teflon) Selfridges, Oxford St, London, or enquiries to Orbit Enterprises, 30 Ross Way, Northwood, Middlesex

Pattern paper*

> MacCulloch and Wallis Ltd, minimum 1 quire (25 sheets)
>
> Metropolitan Sewing Machines

Patterns

> Burda*, Perivale-Gutermann's Ltd, Wadsworth Rd, Greenford, Middlesex UB6 7JS
>
> Knitwit (patterns specially designed for knitted fabrics), 6 High St, Bramley, Guildford, Surrey
>
> McCall*, P.O. Box 27, Athey St, Macclesfield, Cheshire SK11 8EA
>
> Simplicity/Style*, 39–45 Tottenham Court Rd, London W1P 9RD
>
> Vogue/Butterick*, New Lane, Havant, Hampshire PO9 2ND

Poppa range of non-sew snap fasteners*

> Newey-Goodman Ltd, Sedgley Rd West, Tipton, West Midlands

Ribbed fabric for cuffs*

> The Fabric Studio, 10 Frith St, London W1

Showerproof fabrics
> Sixty Plus Textiles, Barley, Nelson, Lancashire
> The Fabric Studio

Simpleframe
> Frame Knitting Ltd, P.O. Box 115, Berkhamsted, Hertfordshire HP4 3TJ

Threads* (large spools of 1000m and above)
> Kinross (Supplies), Oakhill Avenue, Pinner, Middlesex HA5 3DL. Mail-order; will match colours; large stock includes 'fluffy' bulked nylon on 5000m cones.
> MacCulloch and Wallis Ltd

> Molnlycke, Skanthread International, Molnlycke House, Bar Hill, Cambridge CB3 8EJ. Send for list of stockists

Velcro fastening*
> Selectus Ltd, Biddulph, Stoke-on-Trent, ST8 7RH

Vilene*
Interfacings, 'Iron-clean' and other sewing aids
> The Vilene Organisation, P.O. Box No. 3, Greetland, Halifax, West Yorkshire HX4 8NJ
> (Marketed as 'Pellon' in the U.S.A.)

Appendix II

IMPORTERS OF SEWING MACHINES

Bernina
Bogod Machine Co. Ltd, 50–52 Gt Sutton Street, London EC1

Elna
Elna Sewing Machines (G.B.) Ltd, Queen's House, 180/2 Tottenham Court Road, London W1P 9LE

Frister + Rossmann
Frister + Rossmann Sewing Machines Ltd, Mark Way, Swanley, Kent BR8 8NQ

Husqvarna (Viking)
Husqvarna Ltd, P.O. Box 10, Oakley Rd, Luton, Beds. LU4 9QW

Jones-Brother
Jones Sewing Machine Co. Ltd, Shepley Street, Guide Bridge, Audenshaw, Manchester M34 5JD

Pfaff
Pfaff (Britain) Ltd, East Street, Leeds LS9 8EH

Riccar
Riccar (U.K.) Ltd, Riccar House, Nuffield Way, Abingdon, Oxfordshire OX14 1RS

Toyota
Aisin (U.K.) Ltd, Toyota Sewing and Knitting, 34 High Street, Bromley, Kent

See a local classified directory for registered retailers.

Appendix III

**IMPORTERS OF DOMESTIC
OVERLOCKING MACHINES**

Frister-lock and **Frister-Knit-lock**
Frister + Rossmann Sewing Machines Ltd,
Mark Way, Swanley, Kent BR8 8NQ
Homelock
Jones Sewing Machine Co. Ltd, Shepley
Street, Guide Bridge, Audenshaw, Manchester M34 5JD
Huskylock
Husqvarna Ltd, P.O. Box 10, Oakley Rd,
Luton, Beds. LU4 9QW
Wimbledon Sewing Machine Co. Ltd,
308–312 Balham High Road, London
SW17

Kawasaki
Bogod Machine Co. Ltd, 50–52 Gt Sutton
Street, London EC1
Mammylock
Aisin (U.K.) Ltd, Toyota Sewing and
Knitting, 34 High Street, Bromley, Kent
Riccar-Lock
Riccar House, Nuffield Way, Abingdon,
Oxfordshire OX14 1RS

Appendix IV

**SUPPLIERS AND MANUFACTURERS
IN U.S.A.**

General Haberdashery
Newey-Goodman products (including
Poppa-snaps) widely available under
'Newey' brand
Dritz (Scovill), P.O. Box 5028, Spartanburg, S.C. 29304

Interfacings
Pellon Corporation, 119 West 40th St,
New York, N.Y. 10018
Staple Sewing Aids Corp., 141 Lanza
Ave., Garfield, New Jersey 07026
Stacey Fabrics Corp. (A sub. of Shire
National Corp.), 38 Passaic St, Wood-Ridge, New Jersey 07075
Crown Textile Co./Armo, 1412 Broadway, New York, N.Y. 10018

Patterns
Vogue Pattern Service, 161 Sixth
Avenue, New York, N.Y. 10013
Butterick Pattern Service, 161 Avenue of
the Americas, New York, N.Y. 10013
Simplicity Pattern Co. Inc., 200
Madison Ave., New York, N.Y. 10016
The McCall Pattern Co., 230 Park
Avenue, New York

Simpleframe
Inverness Sheep Farm, 3079 Fowlerville
Rd, Caledonia, N.Y. 14423

Threads
Mölnlycke, William E. Wright, South St,
West Warren, MA 01092

Sewing Machines and Overlockers

Swiss Bernina Inc., 534 West Chestnut, Hinsdale, Illinois 60521

Elna Sewing Machines, 11750 Berea Rd, Cleveland, Ohio 44111

Frister + Rossmann, White Sewing Machine Co., Cleveland, Ohio, and Sears Kenmore of Chicago

Husqvarna (Viking), Viking Sewing Machine Co., 2300 Louisiana Ave. North, Minneapolis, Minnesota 55427

Jones-Brother, Brother International Corp., 8 Corporate Place, Piscataway, New Jersey 08854

Pfaff, Pfaff American Sales Corp., 610 Winters Ave., P.O. Box 566, Paramus, New Jersey 07652

Riccar, Riccar America Co., 3184 Pullman St, Costa Mesa, California 92626

Toyota, 333 Sylvan Ave., 1st Floor, Englewood Cliffs, New Jersey 07632

Appendix V

OTHER OVERSEAS SUPPLIERS

Newey-Goodman (general haberdashery) Prym-Newey Ltd, Montreal, Quebec, CANADA
Newey Bros, P.T.Y. Botany, New South Wales, AUSTRALIA
Newey-Goodman Ltd, HONG KONG

Burda Patterns, Aenne Burda, 76 Offenburg, Am Kestendamm 2, GERMANY

Knitwit (patterns for knitted fabrics) 31 Victoria Ave., Castle Mill, Sydney, AUSTRALIA

Frister & Rossmann Sewing Machines and Overlockers
Sears, Toronto, CANADA

Waltons Celestial, Waltons Ltd, Sydney, AUSTRALIA
Empisal, SOUTH AFRICA

Simpleframe

L'atelier, 96 Paris St, Sudbury, Ontario P3E 3E1, CANADA

Frame Knitting (Australia) Pty. Ltd, 58 Neuparth Rd, North Croydon 3136, Melbourne, Victoria, AUSTRALIA
Quicknit, 417 Milner St, Waterkloof, Pretoria, S. AFRICA 0181
Simple Knit Japan Ltd, 1804 Ogawa Higashimachi, Kodaira-shi, Tokyo 187, JAPAN

Appendix VI

FURTHER READING

Cut-and-sew Techniques
Kathleen Kinder's Resource Books. Dalesknit Centre, Settle, Yorkshire

Mary Weaver's *Ribbing Book 1* Weaverknits, Dartford

Mary Weaver's *Book of Machine-knitting Technology and Patterns* Weaverknits, Dartford

Knit Your Own Norwegian Sweaters Dale Yarn Co., Dover, New York and Constable, London

Dressmaking and Tailoring
Reader's Digest Complete Guide to Sewing Reader's Digest Assoc. Ltd, London, New York, Sydney, Cape Town, Montreal

Vogue Sewing Harper and Row, London, Sydney, New York

Sewing Ann Ladbury. Mitchell Beazley Publishers Ltd, London

The Batsford Book of Sewing Ann Ladbury. B. T. Batsford Ltd, London

Fabrics and Fibres
Fabrics Ann Ladbury. Sidgwick and Jackson, London

Fitting
Dress Fitting Natalie Bray. Granada Publishing, London, Sydney, New York, Toronto, Johannesburg and Auckland

Pattern Cutting
Metric Pattern Cutting Winifred Aldrich. Mills and Boon Ltd, London, Toronto and Sydney

Pattern Cutting and Making Up: The Professional Approach 1 Martin Shoben and Janet Ward. B. T. Batsford Ltd, London

Sewing Machines and Overlockers
The Complete Book of the Sewing Machine Angela Thompson, for Women's Institute Books (1980). Also by Book Club Associates with Hamlyn Publishing Co., London, New York, Sydney, Toronto

Magazines
Cut-and-sew articles by Raymonde Chessum in *To and Fro*, a postal club magazine, published from 321 Ashley Road, Parkstone, Poole, Dorset.

Cut-and-sew articles by me in *Knitting Machine Digest*, by post from Hazel Ratcliffe Machine Knitting Services, 142 Frant Road, Thornton Heath, Surrey CR4 7JU

Cut-and-sew articles by me in *Swiftknitters Circular* (British Guild of Machine-knitters) a postal club magazine from Swiftknitters, 131/133 Fratton Road, Portsmouth, Hampshire PO1 5ES

Machine-Knitting News—available from newsagents or by postal subscription from Litharne Ltd, P.O. Box 9, Stratford-on-Avon, Warwickshire CV37 8RS

Knitting Machine Journal—postal club magazine from Alice Wilmhurst, Hawthornes, Whitecroft, Forest of Dean, Gloucestershire, GL15 4PF

INDEX